FINDLEY B. EDGE

The GREENING
of
the
CHURCH

WORD BOOKS, *Publisher*
Waco, Texas

THE GREENING OF THE CHURCH by Findley B. Edge

First Printing—December 1971
Second Printing—April 1972
Third Printing—June 1972
Fourth Printing—September 1973
Fifth Printing—January 1973
Sixth Printing—July 1973
Seventh Printing—March 1974
First Paperback Edition—May 1976
Copyright © 1971 by Word, Incorporated, Waco, Texas 76703

Scripture quotations marked RSV are from the Revised Standard Version of the Bible, copyrighted 1946, 1952, © 1971, 1973 by the Division of Christian Education of the National Council of the Churches of Christ in the U.S.A., and are used by permission.

Printed in the United States of America

ISBN #0-87680-851-8

Library of Congress catalog card number: 70-170911

1. God's Call Mission
2. Evangelism
3. Social Gosp

CONTENTS

PREFACE   9

I. A TIME FOR HOPE   13

    The Church Can Be Renewed   14
    The Church—A Pivotal Battleground   16
    Renewal Is Already Happening   19
    Possible Conflict   20
    Hope and Not Despair   23

Part One

THEOLOGICAL FOUNDATIONS

II. GOD'S CALL TO MISSION   29

    To Be the People of God—What Does It Mean?   30
    Called to Mission   32
    Called to Ministry   37

III. THE NATURE OF GOD'S MISSION   49

    Evangelism and/or Social Action   51
    Inadequacy of Social Emphasis Alone   54
    The Necessity for an Evangelical Emphasis   68
    Cautions for the Evangelical Emphasis   75

IV. THE NATURE OF GOD'S MISSION (continued)   86

    Inadequacy of Evangelical Emphasis Alone   87
    The Necessity for a Social Emphasis   91
    Cautions for the Social Emphasis   100

Part Two

PRACTICAL PROPOSALS

V. MOTIVATION FOR MISSION   107
    Possible Approaches in Seeking Personal Renewal   109
    Personal Discovery through Small Groups   114
    Practical Suggestions for a Searching Group   117

VI. A Practical Program for Mission   135

    How Is a Group "On Mission" Formed   136
    God's Call and My Mission   138
    How Discern God's Call   140
    Types of Mission   144

VII. The Corporate Structure of the Church   161

    Freedom and Variety, Flexibility and Adaptability   161
    Focused Ministry   162
    "Come" Structures and "Go" Structures   163
    Potential Conflict   166
    The Shape of the Organized Church   167
    Groups "On Mission" Related to the Church   170
    Related Questions   174

VIII. The Local Congregation
As a Miniature Theological Seminary   177

    Called to Ministry   177
    The Ministry Accepted   178
    The Function of the Faculty   179
    A Variety of Ministries   180
    A Core Curriculum   181
    Specialized Courses   181
    The Teacher Specializes   182
    Conclusion   188

    APPENDIX—*Resources for Small Groups*   190
    BIBLIOGRAPHY   193

PREFACE

My concern for the renewal of the church has now spanned a decade and a half. Although, as a professor in a theological seminary I have some responsibility for teaching in this general area, this concern has been far more personal than academic. I began to feel a deep sense of despair relative to the church long before I ever heard the word *renewal*. In the intervening years the church has been bombarded with a barrage of criticism. The weaknesses and failures of the church have been catalogued in detail. In my own writing and speaking I contributed my share to this criticism.

There is a growing number today who believe that the negative, critical emphasis has served its day (although the church should never be free from the critical eye of those who love it). The feeling now is that there is need for a positive word with some practical proposals. This book is one effort to contribute to this end. Although I feel the church faces some difficult days ahead, I am no longer filled with despair. In fact I am more filled with hope for the church than I have been in a long time. Chapter one expresses this hope.

There are three major emphases in this book. The first is the conviction that the basic problem in today's church is personal and spiritual. As Charlie Shedd has said, "The problem is not that the churches are filled with empty pews, but that the pews are filled with empty people." We are simply experiencing a spiritual dearth in the life of the churches. Undoubtedly the reasons for this are numerous and complex. However, from my perspective, one fundamental aspect of the problem is that a majority of church members have no clear understanding of who they are or what they are called to be as the "People of God." It is my feeling that the average church member's understanding of "what it means to be a Christian" is so shallow and superficial as to constitute a major perversion of the gospel. It is this misunderstanding—and all that goes with it—that is hindering God's efforts to accomplish his purpose in the world today. Chapter two undertakes to describe from a biblical perspective the essence of God's "call" which Christians must embody if we are to be an expression of God's people in our time.

9

The second emphasis of this book is the conviction that we must recapture a balance between evangelism and social involvement. In its best moments the church has held in balance the social and evangelical aspects of the gospel. This is illustrated in the first three hundred years of the church's history. At times, however, these two have been allowed to clash, as has happened in Protestantism during the past century. One of the great challenges of our generation is to demonstrate again that both evangelism and social involvement can be vigorously and unapologetically pursued. Chapters three and four explore this issue.

The third emphasis has to do with positive, practical proposals. This has become a matter of deep concern to me. There was a time in the recent past when I felt I knew very clearly what was wrong with the church, but my frustration was that I did not know what changes needed to be made or what we needed to start doing in order to bring about improvement. Evidently there were many others in the same predicament because too often in what has been written in the past the emphasis has been on the theological or theoretical or both. Little practical guidance or suggestions have been given as to *how* a church or people might change from what they are to what they ought to become.

We have been told repeatedly that the task of the church is to take the gospel to the marketplaces of life. However, one very practical problem we face is: How do we motivate people to go to the marketplace? Some church members have a level commitment that leads them to be loyal in attending the institutional meetings of the church, but they are unwilling to give the time and energy to become seriously involved in the life of the world. The fact is a number of church members who express a "deep social concern" do more talking than acting. Admittedly this problem of motivation is complex. And I do not claim to know "the answer." This is an area in which the Holy Spirit works, and he works in his own way. However some suggestions concerning motivation are given in chapter five.

The church must also have some organized form. If what it is now doing seems to be inadequate, then how should the church be organized to equip people best for ministry? It must be stated clearly that there is no "one way" by which this change can occur. There are numerous ways in which God is working to bring about change. Likewise, there is no "one program" a church ought to follow. Each church must find its own "shape" or organized life in light of a number of factors. Variety and flexibility are the order of the day. However, a multitude of concerned pastors and laymen who are ready to change cry out for help and for possible guidelines. Chapters six, seven, and eight give some suggestions for these pastors and laymen to consider.

At the outset I want to express my appreciation to Gordon Cosby, pastor of The Church of The Saviour in Washington, D.C. Gordon and I were classmates at Southern Baptist Theological Seminary but it was not until 1964 that we really made "contact." Since that time in renewal conferences he has led at Southern Baptist Theological Seminary, in personal conversations, and during visits to The Church of The Saviour he undoubtedly has influenced my thinking more than any other person. I am indebted also to Keith Miller and others for stimulating insights.

Dr. William E. Hull, dean of the School of Theology and professor of New Testament interpretation, and Dr. E. Glenn Hinson, associate professor of church history, both of Southern Baptist Theological Seminary, and Dr. John R. Claypool, pastor of Broadway Baptist Church, Fort Worth, Texas, were gracious enough to read the entire manuscript and make valuable suggestions. To them I am grateful. In addition I also express appreciation to Mr. Badgett Dillard, director of administration and business manager at Southern Seminary, for tightening up a very loose manuscript and for other assistance in the matter of style. Miss Jean Aiken, office services supervisor, has rendered services to me that were far and above the call of duty. My indebtedness to her is great. I am grateful to Mr. Gene Quinney for typing the final manuscript. Most of all I express appreciation to my wife, Louvenia, for her patience and for the many other things she did to provide me with the freedom and the time needed to complete this manuscript.

December 31, 1970

CHAPTER ONE

A Time for Hope

That there are problems in the modern church cannot be denied! Numerous and loud have been the voices raised in pointing out its weaknesses. My own voice has been raised; therefore I feel I have both the right and the responsibility to express the deep sense of hope I feel for the church at the present time.

The literature dealing with renewal in the church has passed through two stages and hopefully has entered a third. The first stage might be characterized as analytical and critical. This stage lasted from the early 1950s to about 1962. During this time a flood of books appeared that dissected and scrutinized the church from every angle. Obviously this period was almost exclusively negative in nature. The failure of the church was held up for all to see. This attack on the church was so vigorous and sometimes vicious that many came to feel renewal was only negative in its basic thrust. "Criticize the church" came to be popular in speeches, in articles, and in books. A free-lance writer who was having difficulty getting an article published was told by a friend, "If you want to get something published, attack the church!" Each writer seemed to vie with the last in the deft manner in which he expressed his biting, cutting criticisms of the church. It is no wonder that many became "fed up" with this negative emphasis.

The second stage might be characterized as theoretical and theological. During this period the attempt was made to give a more adequate statement as to the nature of the church, primarily from a theological perspective. There were conferences and books that struggled with such questions as: What does it mean to be the church? What is the mission of the church? Is the church mission or does the church have a mission? What does it mean to be a "witnessing community"? What is the relationship of the church to the world? On the basis of the theological answers that began to emerge, some theoretical suggestions were made concerning how the church might express its life. This stage lasted until about 1967.

We have now entered a third stage that may be characterized as positive and practical. A few writers are beginning to give some practical suggestions as to possible solutions for the ills that beset the modern church. This, itself, is a sign of hope. What is needed now is not more criticism but positive proposals that might be considered and tried. During the last decade and a half there has been a considerable amount of "talk" about renewal in the churches. But herein lies a danger. Those of us who are interested in renewal may kill it by talking it to death. Or, we may salve our own consciences in this area of need simply by talking about it. The time has come for action.

THE CHURCH CAN BE RENEWED

There are those who have rejected the institutional church. They say the church cannot be saved. They say the modern church is so bound by tradition, so filled with vested interests, and has so many reactionary members, and such poor leadership that it cannot be used of God to work in today's world. I reject this position. I believe the church can be renewed. Not only do I believe the church can be saved; I believe the church *must* be saved! This is not to say that the church with its present organizational structures will continue. Organizational structure has always been a changing factor in the life of the church. No one knows what the structures of the future church may be. But one of the great challenges we face will be to discover what some of these structures might be. Even these future structures will eventually become outmoded. But I believe the "new" that God is working in the world today can and will take place *within* the institutional church rather than from outside the church.

A number of these para-ecclesial agencies have sprung up in recent years. Many who had become disillusioned with the church found meaning and dynamic within such agencies. A comic strip pictured two small boys in conversation. One was saying to the other, "We don't belong to a church anymore. We belong to a coffeehouse." These new experimental forms outside the institutional church, in most instances, serve a positive and useful purpose. They are small and flexible and thus more free to experiment than is the traditional church. They are free to fail as well as free to succeed. In this way they are able to discover paths which the church might desire to follow. They prod the church; they stimulate the church; they sit in judgment upon the church; they challenge the church; they give insights to the church.

However, I am convinced that none of these para-ecclesial agencies, valuable as they are, will become the "pattern" which God will choose to accomplish his purpose in the world in our time. For one thing, these agencies enlist their adherents or participants by skimming the members from some local churches. These agencies rarely recruit any of their "members" from the "world," that is, from those who have never been related to the church. Granted that the church has been far from perfect in recent years, yet at some point these people were recruited and taught enough gospel that they were able to recognize that the church was not what it ought to be. If it were not for the disillusioned church people, these new experimental ministries would be hard-pressed to find participants. I am convinced that these agencies do not provide the "wave" of the future.

Even some of those who had given up on the institutional church a few years ago are now beginning to change their minds. For example, when Stephen C. Rose was editor of *Renewal Magazine,* he was listed among the "radicals." He was viewed as one of the "angry young men." He edited a book entitled *Who's Killing the Church?*[1] In giving an explanation of the title in the preface he said there are three possible answers to the question. First, there is the possibility that man and the forces of a secular world are killing the church. Humanism is so rampant; materialism has so come to dominate the life of man; evil of every description has become so powerful in our time that these forces are simply overwhelming the church. There is a second group who say that the forces of the world can never become sufficiently powerful to kill the church. Their answer is that the church is dying from within because of apathy, neglect, and indifference. Because the church refuses to take the world and its needs seriously, she finds herself slowly dying. The verdict of the second group is that the church is committing suicide. The third answer grows out of the second but is quite distinct from it. A new wine is being fermented. Old forms are being broken. New life is coming into being—the old is dying. God is killing the church! The old forms must die in order that the new might be born.

It is difficult to say whether Rose would place himself in group two or group three. However, in his own book *The Grass Roots Church,* in which he makes his own practical proposal for the life of the church, he said, "The idea of giving up on the institutional Church is most tempting to me and to many others. . . . But . . . we owe the Church the obligation of trying to develop institutional relevance before summarily jettisoning the institution. We must, at least for now, place renewal and restructuring ahead of total rejection of the institution."[2]

I believe the church can be renewed because it provides us with the greatest reservoir of people committed to God that can be found anywhere. Granted that there are many unregenerate people within the church. Granted that there is apathy, neglect, and indifference within the church. Granted that the church is introverted, that she is more concerned with her own welfare than with the welfare of the world. Granted that the church is irrelevant. Say the worst you can about the church. Still, it is within the church that one finds the most people who are sensitive and can be led to be sensitive to the radical call of God and to what God is doing in the world today. Granted also that some of these people have become so disillusioned with the church they have left it. Granted, too, that there are some people who have never been related to the church who would be willing to give themselves to God and to what he is doing. These say, "Jesus, yes; the church, no." But in terms of strategy, I am convinced that it is within the church we will find the greatest number of potential recruits for the "new" that God seems to be doing in our time. When the church begins to "get with it" more, these others will also become potential recruits.

Finally, I believe the church must be renewed because, if this happens, then that which God is seeking to do in the world will be thrust forward in a far more effective and extensive manner than in any other single way. Some sincere and earnest people have given up on the church and left it. I must confess that in my time of despair and disenchantment with the church this also crossed my mind. But then I began to cast about for options to fulfill that which I felt God was seeking to accomplish. Several possibilities suggested themselves and were explored. Each one had some potential. But when I looked at these possibilities in light of what could happen if the church were really to "come alive," there simply was no comparison. For these reasons I am committed to the renewal of the church.

THE CHURCH—A PIVOTAL BATTLEGROUND

I believe in the church because what happens to and in the church is supremely important. Ultimately the "battleground" for the Christian is in the world. It is the world for which Christ died. It is the world to which we as Christians are sent. We must never lose this focus. However, what ultimately happens in the world depends upon what first happens in the local church. Is there in the local congregation a people who are alive and committed? Is there a people who are sensitive and available? In his great priestly prayer, our Lord prayed, "For their sakes I sanctify myself" (John 17:19). In effect he was saying, "For their sakes I set myself apart for God's use." At this particular point Jesus was concentrating upon himself. Nor was this selfish, because what was going to happen for the world depended upon how he reacted in the next few hours. In like manner, for the sake of the world it is necessary to concentrate first upon the church —upon her life and dynamic. Nor is this selfish, because what happens to the world will depend in large measure upon what has first happened in local congregations.

During 1964 and 1965, it was my privilege to visit and study the German evangelical academies. These are conference centers that grew up after the Second World War in a valiant effort to bridge the gap between the church and the world. I was deeply impressed with what I saw in that they were really trying to be a "servant people." They let the "world write the agenda." Whatever the need, they were there to serve. They were deeply committed to the world. However, I saw what I felt was a tragic flaw. They gave themselves with abandon to serving the world, but almost none of them made any effort to minister to the church. That is, they sought to renew the world, but did not make a corresponding effort to renew the church. When I asked about this, their reply was, "The church is not renewable."

I certainly do not want to be critical because I think I understand something of the difficulty they confronted. But when I asked if ever there were people who were really "turned on" during one of their conferences, they answered in the affirmative. Then I asked, "What happens when they leave the conference?" Time and again the person with whom I was talking would simply shake his head and admit that they did not go back to a church because the churches really could not minister meaningfully to them. An effort is made to put them in touch with others who had been to one of the conferences. Or they would try to keep in touch through a monthly paper that is sent out. Or one of the leaders in the conference would make an annual visit to try to keep in touch. But the thought kept coming to

me, "How are these who have 'come alive' to be ministered to on a
continuing basis? This is the task of the local church. Granted that
the present church is in dire circumstances, but why don't they seek
to renew the church with the same selfless, reckless abandon that they
have in seeking to renew the world?" They served the world whether
it was renewable or not—risking rejection and failure, but they were
unwilling to serve the church on the same terms.

This seemed to be very poor strategy. How were they to help individuals conserve whatever of meaning happened to them during one
of the conferences? How did they hope to make any significant and
continuing impact upon the world? There needs to be a base from
which the people of God invade the world . . . a place of continuing
fellowship . . . a place where those who are "coming alive" are taught
and equipped. And there needs to be someone to teach and equip
them.

It seems to me the strategy of Laurence Byers with his motorcycle
ministry in Berkeley, California, is much the better. In struggling with
the problem of where his own ministry could best be expressed, he
reflects upon those of the laity who minister in the real world of riots,
courtrooms, and dingy flats. Then he says, "Perhaps I could join such
people in that world and get away from the phonies who want to
substitute 'church work' for the work of the church! But if I joined
such laity in the working world, who would be there to nurture them
in the gospel to enable them better to apply it to life? There was still
a need for the local pastor—somewhere! . . . Perhaps I should recon-
sider my resignation! Maybe God was renewing his church from
within."[3] What happens to the world depends in part upon what has
already happened to the *laos* of God.

Thus, to renew the present church is the imperative challenge of
today. To serve God in a local church is a high and holy calling. Yet,
unfortunately, there are many ministers who are leaving the local
church ministry. Undoubtedly in some instances there are valid
reasons, but for the most part, it may simply be a means of escape.
They are willing to suffer pain in a ghetto ministry, but are unwilling
to endure the pain and agony of loving sinners within the church. It
is apparently easier to love and forgive sinners in the ghetto than it is
to love and forgive them in the church! I agree completely with Jud,
"So, hats off to pastors who have coats off to the future, who are
staying at their posts, willing to bear the heat of the day! Not too
long ago it was a sign of courage and vision to leave the pastorate

and, while fully committed to the gospel, seek secular employment. Now, I say, it is a sign of courage and vision to stay and help lead the church through this period of change to a new and faithful stance."[4]

In the seminaries it seems there have been an inordinate number of students who are pointing toward some nonchurch type of ministry, such as teaching. Certainly teaching is a valid and needed ministry. I wouldn't question the motives of anyone who plans to enter the teaching ministry. Yet I cannot help but feel that the attractiveness of teaching is increasing because the glamor of the local church as a place of service is decreasing.

Obviously each person must find his place of ministry under the leadership of the Holy Spirit. It is my judgment, however, that the local church presents one of the pivotal battlegrounds and one of the key opportunities for ministry in our time. A call to the local church may be a call to the most difficult spot—more difficult than a call to the world. It may be to the church that God is calling his most able men and women—that is, those most able to love, to suffer, to forgive, to be reviled and rejected yet continue to pray for those who despitefully use them.

RENEWAL IS ALREADY HAPPENING

I have hope for the church because it is already being renewed. A few years ago we could count on the fingers of one hand the churches in which something dynamic and exciting was occurring. Now there are literally thousands of churches where something is happening. They are of all denominations and types—large, small, inner city, suburban, rural, county seat. Granted, in most instances they are taking only the first, faltering steps, but they give promise of that which is to come.

What is emerging? Do not be deceived into thinking that the change is primarily organizational. Don't entertain the mistaken notion that devising new approaches or changing programs will bring about renewal and new life in the church. It is so easy to mistake form for essence, to mistake the external for the internal. When we see "new life" break out in some church, our tendency is to adopt their program and expect it to produce life. It simply doesn't happen that way. Life and dynamic must have some structure in the church, but structure does not automatically produce life and dynamic.

The word that I believe characterizes the major weakness in the life of the present church is *superficial*. Too many churchmen have only a superficial relationship with God, a superficial understanding of who God is and what he is about in the world, a superficial commitment to God, a superficial concern for the world, and a superficial involvement in the work God is doing in the world.

What is happening that gives me hope? In the lives of a growing number of people that which was secondhand has become firsthand! What was external has become internal! What was conceptual has become personal! What was propositional has become experiential! What was routine and habitual has become exciting! People are having experiences with God in such fashion that they are beginning to talk about what God is doing in their lives now! They are becoming sensitive to and concerned about and involved in the lives of others and of society! Those who have met God at one level of their lives are coming to meet him at a deeper level, and their lives are being transformed! Consequently, those who have leadership responsibility must understand that if new life is to break out in the churches, the focus must be on persons!

POSSIBLE CONFLICT

Along with an expression of hope it is necessary to make a realistic appraisal of potential conflict that may be encountered. It would seem that with "spiritual" objectives such as the ones just expressed, there would be no difficulty securing common agreement within the church. But unfortunately, this is not the case. Actually it is when these "spiritual" objectives are spelled out in terms of specifics that difficulties and opposition arise.

In this one area I wish that my analysis of the present situation were erroneous. However, I have come to feel that renewal in the church will not take place without pain and conflict. This conflict stems from a variety of sources. First, there are those who feel that what the church is now doing, while not perfect, is precisely what the church ought to be doing. They do not understand why all this criticism of the church is being expressed. Indeed, they feel that those who are expressing criticism are among the major enemies of the church. Furthermore they believe this criticism has a serious and detrimental effect on the life and work of the church. It is their contention that if we would stop all this negative talk, get back in the church, put our shoulders to the wheel and push harder, we could stop the decline of the church and push her forward once again. They insist that the effectiveness of the principles being used in the churches was demonstrated in the great upsurge during the 1950s and that they would work again if only we would work them. We don't need anything "new," we simply need to go back to the tried and proven principles we already have. Thus anything "new" is going to come into conflict with this group.

There is a second group with whom there is potential conflict. These are people who simply do not want to change. They point out that change is taking place all about us. There is change in international relations. There is change in politics . . . in business . . . in society. There is unrest on university campuses and violence in the streets. These people are overwhelmed by the massive change all about them. So they cry, "Let's have at least one place where there is no change. Let's have one place where we can find some security. Let's have one place where we can have some measure of peace." In the midst of turmoil, this desire for the familiar and for peace is certainly understandable. These people recognize that there is little they can do to stop the changes taking place in business or to stem the tide of change in society. But, they say, there is one place where we can stop these changes—and that is in church. So when the call for something "new" is introduced, it becomes the source of serious problems.

The third group presents an even more serious problem. This is the group for whom a serious understanding of the call of God constitutes a real threat. These people already have all the religion they want. They believe in God, in a measure. They are faithful to the church, up to a point. They try to do right by their fellow-man, in general. Their religion is "under control." They don't believe a man ought to be a religious fanatic. He ought to take his religion seriously, but not too seriously. And, if he supports the work of the church with his money and attends on Sunday morning, what more could God expect? He was baptized as a baby and later confirmed, or he "made a profession of faith," or whatever his denomination told him he was supposed to do—so God is now bound to take care of him, here and hereafter. Satisfied with what he is doing, he is determined not to do anything else.

Into this setting come a group of people talking about "total commitment" . . . about being "ministers of God" . . . about "radical obedience" . . . about "involvement and giving your life for others."

This kind of talk simply doesn't make sense to our friend in this third group. He thinks this is a bunch of nonsense, and he is certain that this is carrying religion too far. But the "total commitment" people say this is the very essence of God's call to his people. They insist that anything less is inadequate and unacceptable. If they are serious and persistent in pressing this "new" claim of God, then our friend has one of two choices. Either he must be converted to their understanding of the Christian faith and join with them, or he must find some way of defending his present understanding of religion. This becomes a most serious issue with him because he is threatened at a pivotal point in his life—his religion. He does have a concern about his relation with God and about his eternal destiny. But all that is human within him rebels against this "new" that is being presented to him. Therefore his natural tendency will be to lash out against the "new." If possible, he will try to defeat it intellectually, on a rational basis. But if this is not successful, he will try to defeat it by ridicule. Holding these people up to scorn before his friends inside and outside the church, he will laugh at them as being a "bunch of Holy Joes." And if this fails, he will lash out by using certain "labels" against them: "Communists," "liberals," or "fundamentalists" (whichever is the worst in his particular area). But this is a most serious matter for him. Somehow he must convince himself that the religion he has, and his expression of it, is adequate and satisfactory. Since he certainly is not planning to make any changes in himself, anything that threatens his status quo is in peril.

Finally, there are those in our churches who with genuineness and intelligence are convinced that this new emphasis is erroneous. Indeed, even those who seem committed to the "new" that is happening in the church today are not agreed as to major matters of theology and practice. So their opponents contend that this "new" which is so vigorously advocated is only one person's view of religion or one group's understanding of the nature and meaning of the Christian life. Therefore, they, with serious commitment and with intelligent investigation, are convinced that what they hear as the "new" being advocated is wrong and detrimental to the church and to its ministry in today's world. They feel compelled to oppose, and rightly so, that which they believe to be erroneous.

What then might be the outcome of this potential conflict? Of course, no one can forecast with any degree of certainty what the future will be. However, from one perspective, it seems that the conflict—or at least this confrontation—is inevitable because some of us are convinced that the present expression of the life of the church is unfaithful to God. It is an incomplete expression of the gospel and an inadequate instrument for God to use in his redemptive purpose in our time. Therefore, on the basis of our commitment to God and of our understanding of the Christian faith, we feel a deep, compelling sense of urgency to confront the church with this understanding of the Christian faith and the Christian way. We feel that this must be done from within the church, and it is not our intention to get out of the church. Whether we are led by the Holy Spirit or by some alien spirit, perhaps only time will tell. I don't mean to imply that I feel there is no fault or error in our understanding of the Christian way. But what I am saying is that we feel an impelling from deep within, therefore we must speak! This confrontation is necessary. We cannot hold our peace for the sake of peace!

Hopefully, this confrontation will be done in the spirit of Christ and will lead to a minimum of conflict. If and when this conflict does come, again, hopefully, we will deal with it maturely as Christians and not as unbelievers. It is possible for us to use conflict creatively and positively, and out of it may come something that is better than we knew or had before. But remembering Jesus' conflict with the religious leaders of his day, we must face the fact that confrontation may lead to pain and suffering.

Hope and Not Despair

In spite of difficulties within and without the church, this is a time for hope and not despair. Even such an unlikely thing as the rebellion of modern youth may, in reality, be a real sign of hope. My generation provided modern youth with "everything that money could buy." But we failed to provide for or minister to their inner needs, and we did not give ourselves to them. This rebellion of youth has caused some of us to reflect upon the fact that we placed an overemphasis upon materialism. From a religious perspective this caused our understanding of and commitment to the Christian faith to get out of perspective. An increasing number are becoming aware that for a person to have a house, good clothes, two cars, and to climb the organizational ladder (by whatever means is necessary) is not the ultimate goal of existence.

Likewise, for several generations the Puritan ethic has made a meaningful and significant contribution to personal morality, and personal morality is highly desirable. The rugged individualism of the frontier days has also contributed to our personal ethic, giving us ambition and determination. These two ingredients, in the main, produced a middle-class society in which each person took care of himself and expected everyone else to do the same. But the Puritan ethic and rugged individualism do not constitute the whole of the Christian ethic.

We have a chance now to recapture the biblical emphasis, "Thou shalt love thy neighbor as thyself," and I am "my brother's keeper." We are coming to recognize that there are reasons other than laziness why people are in poverty, want, and need. We see that hopelessness breeds laziness, but regardless of the particular situation a person is in, God loves him, and we must be agents of that love. The world is teaching us what the Holy Spirit should have been able to teach us long ago, namely, we are living in one world—God's world. No one of us can be completely whole so long as anyone about us is broken.

This is a time for hope! It is true that the church faces difficulties that are serious and complex, however it is so easy for us to forget the lessons taught by church history. The renewal of the church ultimately is the work of God, and there is growing evidence that God is at work renewing his church today. This is neither the first nor the most serious difficulty the church has confronted in its long history. We who live today may sometimes have the feeling that the whole of the church is crumbling about us, but we forget those daring Christians of other years who heroically faced far more serious difficulties than we now face and emerged victorious. For the church, periods of difficulty have frequently been times of challenge and opportunity. The church has made its greatest impact upon society, not when the church was large, rich, and at ease, but rather when it consisted of a people who were committed to God in spite of all the difficulties they confronted.

It is this type of church that seems to be emerging. Small groups of committed Christians are springing up everywhere. The ecumenical nature of these groups, the breakdown of many of the superficial barriers that have divided, the increasing concern for the physical and social welfare of people—all combine to give real hope. We stand on the threshold of advance. There looms before us a real possibility of a resurgence in the realm of the spiritual in our time—if we are daring enough to become a part of it. What is it God is seek-

ing to do and what is the nature of our response to his call? To this
we now turn our attention.

NOTES

1. Stephen C. Rose, ed., *Who's Killing the Church?* (Chicago: Chicago
City Missionary Society, 1966).

2. Stephen C. Rose, *The Grass Roots Church* (New York: Holt, Rinehart & Winston, 1966), pp. 24, 26.

3. Laurence P. Byers, *Christians in Crossfire* (Philadelphia: Westminster
Press, 1967), pp. 132–33.

4. Gerald J. Jud, *Pilgrim's Process* (Philadelphia: United Church Press,
1967), p. 65.

PART ONE

Theological Foundations

CHAPTER TWO

God's Call to Mission

It was during my first year as a seminary student that I was confronted with the striking similarity of the Pharisaism of Jesus' day and the religious life of Protestantism. The people in the churches were what I would call good people. Indeed they were the best people in the communities of which they were a part. The problem, as I saw it, was that in the churches we were simply "going through the motions." We were constantly trying to pump some life into meetings which seemed to be listless and lifeless. It was dull routine. In my youthful idealism I was deeply disturbed by what I saw and felt. As a pastor of a small rural church, I did the only thing I knew to do—I preached a sermon on it. I put together all of my feelings about the spiritual dynamic of the gospel and our seeming failure to appropriate and express it. I still remember the intensity I felt on that Sunday morning. I don't know what I expected to happen, but I wasn't prepared for what did happen—nothing, absolutely nothing! After the sermon the people filed by, shook my hand, and told me they enjoyed it, and that was it!

This shook me rather deeply, but my concern did not die. I stayed for graduate study, and in my doctoral dissertation I explored the problem of institutionalism. I wanted to find out why the church throughout its history tended to become institutionalized and why people let religion become formal, external, lifeless, and routine. I discovered what to me were some meaningful insights. However, this was just at the conclusion of the Second World War and the beginning of the great "upsurge in religion" that followed. Like most everyone else, I was caught up in this period of expansion and growth.

I really don't remember when the first gnawing questions again began to raise their ugly heads in my mind. It seems to me that it was sometime around the mid 1950s. I know it was related to the racial situation. When the first "sit-ins" and marches were held, I felt this was an opportunity for the churches to rise up and really give a witness that God is "no respecter of persons." I felt here was a chance for Christians to demonstrate their commitment to Christ rather than to culture. But instead of witness I found only silence, or worse, negative reaction.

I am aware, of course, that the racial issue does not constitute the whole of the gospel, but this was the straw that broke the camel's back for me. Churches of all denominations were experiencing phenomenal growth numerically, budgets were soaring, buildings were being built. We were enlisting people, teaching and training them—but for what? I said to myself, "If this is all the gospel is, if this is all the church is about, then I'm not sure this is what I want to give my life to." We would have our meetings at church and talk about loving God and talk about saving the world—and I would think about the racial situation. The more I went to church, the more meetings I sat in, the more I became "fed up" with all the "talk" the church was doing—with no action. At this time I began to wonder if it would not be better for me to stay away from church. The little religion I built up during the week, I lost on Sunday.

Then I started thinking of the Pharisees. They thought they had appropriated in a meaningful way "the Faith of their Fathers," but our Lord said, "You've missed it!" And I thought, "Here we are. We think we have appropriated and are expressing in a meaningful way 'the Faith of our Fathers.' But I suspect that if our Lord were again on earth in the flesh he would say to us, 'Man, you've missed it! You've just missed it.' " And I didn't want to be a part of something that was missing it. On the other hand, I was convinced that there was reality behind the church and what it was trying to do. I said to myself, "If we have missed it, if we have let this reality slip through our fingers, what *is* the reality?" That's when I started on my own quest.[1]

TO BE THE PEOPLE OF GOD—WHAT DOES IT MEAN?

A phrase that came to have deep meaning for me during this period is one of the phrases Paul used to designate the church, namely, "the People of God." I was aware that God was calling to himself a unique people, but what was the essence of their uniqueness? How is this uniqueness to be expressed? What is the unique distinction between the People of God and "the rest of the world"? At one time, as I was growing up, I thought that the uniqueness of God's People was that they were "good." But I came to find out that there were a lot of "good" people in the world who made no claim to being "God's People." I am convinced that God's People are supposed to be "good," but if good people are not necessarily God's People, then what is the difference between good people and God's People?

I was struggling with the basic question of the Christian Faith— *What really does it mean to be the People of God?* I didn't know the answer to this question—not with certainty and clarity. *This is the basic problem in the life of the modern church.* We don't know who we are or what we are supposed to be as the People of God! I am convinced that a majority of both laymen and clergy do not know the answer to this question—not with clarity. This is not the only problem of the church, but it is the central problem.

Our problem is not primarily that attendance statistics are declining or that the budget is becoming increasingly difficult to raise. It is that we do not know who we are or what we are called to be as the People of God. We do not know how to be an expression of the People of God because we really don't know what it means *to be* the People of God. If it means something more than or something other than "being good," "believing in Jesus," and "being faithful to the church," then most of us don't know what it is. I would like to share with you my answer to this question, because it has been the single most influential factor in my life in the last few years. This answer has given shape and direction to my recent ministry, and it has brought back meaning and excitement for me in the ministry. This is the "reality" for which I was searching.

When I began asking myself with seriousness what it really meant to be the People of God, other questions also came. Why was God calling a people in the first place? What was he calling them to? What was he calling them for? If I could get the answers to these questions, then I might have a clue to the answer to my basic question. My quest took me to the Bible. As much as I could, I wanted to find out what God had to say in answer to these questions. So this led me back to the beginning when man of his own free, voluntary action sinned and separated himself from God. And God, on his part, set about his purpose of bringing man back into a valid relationship with himself.

CALLED TO MISSION

The question is: How is God going to accomplish this divine, eternal purpose? Being God he could have sent angels to be the instruments of his purpose. He could have caused the very stones to cry out and be his witnesses. But instead he chose another plan. He began by calling a man. We have an account of this in Genesis 12:1-3. "Now the Lord had said unto Abram, Get thee out of thy country, and from thy kindred, and from thy father's house, unto a land that I will show thee: . . . and thou shalt be a blessing: And I will bless them that bless thee, and curse him that curseth thee: and in thee shall all families of the earth be blessed."[2]

We find at least two things in these verses. First, there is God's purpose stated, "All families of the earth are to be blessed." That is, all people everywhere are to come to know God as loving Father. This is what God is now about. He is working to restore a relationship that has been broken. God is seeking to bring wholeness to people, indeed to his whole created order. This can be accomplished only through an intimate relationship with him in which man lets God be God in his life. We call it reconciliation and redemption. This is God's purpose. This is what God is about.

In the second place, we find God's plan for the accomplishment of this purpose—God says to Abraham, "You are to be a blessing." The significant thing we need to note here is that God's basic call to Abraham was a call to a task! It was a call to a mission. It is true that God said, "I will bless you." Thus, in the call there is a receiving and an accepting. But the essence of the call is to engage in something with God and for God.

Let's come at it from a slightly different perspective. Why was God calling a people in the first place? He was calling a people because there was a brokenness between himself and his creation, and he was calling an instrument in whom and through whom he could work to bring man back to himself. This is why God was calling Abraham, and this is the purpose for which he called him. It was this call to mission that was at the center of the covenant into which God entered with Abraham. It is true that God's promise of "gift" is very real—"I will bless you." But the reason God was calling Abraham in the first place was that he was engaged in a mighty eternal purpose, and he was calling a man to give his life as an instrument in whom and through whom God could work to accomplish this redemptive mission. It was as man understood the call to mission and gave God his life to be an instrument of this mission that God was able to shower upon him the gift and the blessings he was offering. *The gift and the call are inseparable.* A person cannot have one without the other.

This covenant was repeated with Abraham's son, Isaac, and with Isaac's son, Jacob. And years later in Exodus 19:3-8 we have an account of God's reaffirmation of his initial covenant. "And Moses went up unto God, and the Lord called unto him out of the mountain, saying, Thus shalt thou say to the house of Jacob, and tell the children of Israel; Ye have seen what I did unto the Egyptians, and how I bare you on eagles' wings, and brought you unto myself." To paraphrase, God says to Moses, go back to the people and say to them, "Look, you have seen what I did to the Egyptians, how miraculously I delivered you from the pit of death. You have seen how I have led you and cared for you and protected you as though you were a helpless eaglet on the wings of a mighty eagle. You have seen a demonstration of my love for you. You have seen a demonstration of my might and power. You have seen who I AM!"

Continuing now with verses 5-8, "Therefore, if [notice the condition] ye will obey my voice indeed, and keep my covenant, then ye shall be a peculiar treasure unto me above all people: for all the earth is mine: And ye shall be unto me a kingdom of priests, and a holy nation. These are the words which thou shalt speak unto the children of Israel. . . . And all the people answered together, and said, All that the Lord hath spoken we will do."

Thus God and the people entered into a covenant relationship. God called them to be his people. Again, there is a very pivotal point that must be noted. God's basic call was to a mission, to a task. To repeat our fundamental question, why was God calling a people in the first place? What was he calling them for and what was he calling them to? God was engaged in a redemptive task in the world, and he was calling a people who would give their lives to join with him in this redemptive mission. Thus God's basic call to his people is a call to mission, not a call to receive something or to accept something.

He said to them, you "shall be to me a kingdom of priests." One of the functions of a priest is to be a mediator, to stand between God and man and seek to bring the two together. God says in effect, "I am calling you to be my special people for my special purpose. (This is far more than just 'being good,' though of course I expect you to be 'good.') I am calling you to be a kingdom of priests, a people of priests. Your function is in terms of my redemptive purpose. You are to be instruments to seek to bring man and God together. This is why I am calling you. It is to this mission I am calling you. Will you do it?" And all the people said, "We will do it!"

But, as so often happens, they misunderstood the nature of their call. They thought that God had called them primarily to bless them. They thought God had called them simply to be in some special relationship with him as his people—that he had called them primarily to give them something. And so they took God—accepted him—as their own possession. But they misunderstood why they were called and the purpose of their call. And thus they failed to carry out the purpose of their call. In the Old Testament God, through his prophets and in other writings, came time and time again to the people to try to get them to understand the true nature of why they were called and to what they were called. But they failed to understand or to carry out the purpose of their calling.

In the fullness of time, Jesus came. In Matthew 21 there are two parables told by our Lord. The first is the parable of two sons. To paraphrase, Jesus said, a certain man had two sons. The father came to the first and said, "Son, go work today in my vineyard." And he answered, "I will not." But afterward he repented and went. Then he came to the second son and said the same thing, "Son, go work today in my vineyard." This son replied, "I go, sir." But he did not go. The second son symbolizes Israel. God had called Israel to be his People. He had called them for the purpose of redemption and to be a "kingdom of priests," a people who would give their lives to the purpose of bringing man and God together. God said to the people, Israel, "Go work today in my vineyard." And they said, "We will do it." But they didn't. They failed.

In the call of God, gift and demand are inexorably intertwined. There is certainly gift, because God desires to give himself to people. But there is also demand. A person cannot have one without the other. The grace that saves is a "costly grace," as Bonhoeffer has reminded us. And the demand is in terms of understanding and accepting mission—God's mission. As Emil Brunner says, "One who receives this Word, and by it salvation, receives along with it the duty of passing this Word on. . . . Where there is no mission, there is no Church, and where there is neither Church nor mission, there is no faith."[3]

In the parable of the two sons we have another illustration of Israel's tragic misunderstanding of the nature of God's call as evidenced by the reaction of the Pharisees. Now, I have no desire to paint an unfair picture of the Pharisees. They were the "choicest spirits of the Judaism of Jesus' day." Actually, they were a highly moral people, deeply dedicated to religion as they understood it. Coming into existence because the average Israelite was not keeping the commandments of God with care and devotion, the Pharisees were a small group who "separated" themselves from the "common people" and dedicated themselves to the strict observance of God's law. Indeed this is precisely the point of their misunderstanding of God's call. They thought God had called them to be a *separated people* rather than a *people on mission*. The danger the churches face today is exactly this same misunderstanding.

The fact is, Judaism had an evangelistic thrust. Throughout the Graeco-Roman world they sought proselytes to the Jewish faith (Matt. 23:15a). However, theirs was a type of exclusive evangelism—an evangelism on their own terms. They would accept those who were willing to become "separated" from the world and who would give themselves with devoted concern to institutional observance and ceremonial purity. But they did not understand that they were called by God to be instruments of his caring love—thrust into the world, not separated from the world—to love people where they were and as they were. The Pharisees were willing to welcome "sinners" *after* they repented. The revolutionary demonstration of Jesus was that he loved "sinners" *before* they repented. This is the way God loves, and this is the way God is calling his people to love. To love like this is their mission because it is God's mission.

The second parable in Matthew begins in verse 33. To paraphrase again, the parable tells about a certain man who built a vineyard and let it out to workers. He went into a far country. When the time of harvest came, he sent some of his servants to receive the fruits of it. But the workers in the vineyard stoned or killed these servants. The owner of the vineyard sent still more servants and they were stoned and killed also. Finally the owner of the vineyard said, "I know what I will do. I will send my son. Surely these people will reverence my son." But the workers in the vineyard heard that the son was coming, and they said, "Let's kill him and take the whole thing for ourselves." Jesus turned to the people who were standing around and said, "Now tell me, what do you think the owner of the vineyard will do to these

workers in the vineyard?" They replied, "Why, he will destroy these
evil men."

Then follows what I consider to be one of the most pivotal, important, and significant verses in all of the Bible. Jesus is speaking to
the scribes and Pharisees who are the official representatives of
Judaism. God and Israel are once again facing each other in direct
confrontation. Jesus says, "Therefore say I unto you, The kingdom of
God shall be taken from you, and given to a nation bringing forth the
fruits thereof" (Matt. 21:43). There are serious and complicated
theological questions involved in these words.[4] But we cannot escape
the fact that Jesus did say to Israel that the kingdom was to be taken
from them and another people was going to be called. In effect Jesus
said to Israel, for more than a thousand years you have had your
chance. God called you for a purpose. God said, go work in my vineyard. Be a kingdom of priests. You said you would do it, but you
failed. Therefore, the kingdom is taken from you and given to a
people who *will* bring forth fruit—that is, who will fulfill the purpose
of their calling.

God calls the "new" Israel, and you and I make the audacious
claim that we are a part of this "new" Israel of God. But the thing
we must understand with clarity is, the "new" Israel is called for precisely the same purpose as was the original Israel. Basic in our call
is a call to a task. *We are called to a mission.* God is not calling us
simply to give us something. Those who emphasize "belief" as the
whole aspect of salvation need to note that in the parable of the two
sons, in the parable of the owner of the vineyard, in the parable of
the last judgment, not one word was said about belief. Of course "belief" is involved, but the emphasis is placed here on the results, the
fruits, the expression of valid "belief." The people involved were not
rejected because they did not believe but because they failed to fulfill
the purpose for which they were called. This is why God is calling his
people. This is to what he is calling his people, and this is the real
mission of the church!

What really does it mean to be the People of God? They are a
people who believe, certainly. They are a people who are "good" in
terms of personal morality, certainly. But these things do not constitute the heart of the matter. The uniqueness of God's people is that
they are called to a mission. This is clearly understood. They have
joyfully accepted this mission and have given their lives to its fulfillment.

This mission in which God is engaged is redemptive. It is both personal and social. The People of God believe that what God is seeking to do in the lives of people and in the world is what is desperately needed. They believe this so deeply and with such commitment that their lives are joyfully given to God as instruments in seeking to cause the will of God to be "done on earth as it is in heaven." This is the nature of their uniqueness. In living life this way, in losing their lives for the gospel's sake, they find that Jesus is absolutely correct—in their own lives they begin to find healing, wholeness, meaning, blessings, life in increasing abundance!

It seems to me that the sin of Israel is being repeated today. So many church members have come to God for what they can get out of him. Too often they haven't the slightest idea, or even the slightest concern, as to what it really means to be God's people. If renewal is to take place in our churches, it must begin right at this point—there must be a fundamental change in persons! It is imperative that we become a people who understand who we are, who God is, what God is about in the world and what God is calling us to be about in the world. It is true we need some new programs and some new approaches in our churches, but the fundamental need is for a new people! The basic problem in the churches is spiritual, and this must be met before any real or significant change will take place in the world. Changing organizations or programs simply will not get the job done!

On the other hand we do not have to speculate on what God does to a people who misunderstand and who fail to carry out the purpose of his calling. He has already demonstrated this in his dealing with Israel. God is serious about the redemptive mission in which he is engaged in the world. On his part, he has gone the limit; "He that spared not his own Son . . ." (Rom. 8:32). God will not view lightly a people who respond to his call with their lips but fail to fulfill this mission. His dealing with the first Israel should stand as a blazing warning as to what happens to a people who fail to understand and fulfill the purpose of his call.

CALLED TO MINISTRY

Anyone even casually related to the church is aware that it has come upon hard times. This is a rather strange phenomenon because the church today has more members than ever before to do its work, and they are better educated than they have ever been. In addition, the church has more money and better buildings and equipment. It has a superb understanding of educational techniques and has at its disposal the means of mass communications. But in spite of all of this, church work is declining in many areas.

Why? The answer, I am sure, is both difficult and complex. Numerous forces touch and influence the church today. However, I would like to suggest two reasons that I feel play a most significant part in the difficulties which the church is experiencing. First, the church is facing problems because its work is being done primarily by the wrong people. And, I believe the church is experiencing difficulty because its work is being done in the wrong place.

1. The Wrong People

These two answers—the wrong people and the wrong place—demand an explanation. This leads us to a consideration of the doctrine of the priesthood of all believers. This has received considerable attention in recent years, but, unfortunately, its full meaning and significance is still not adequately understood. The doctrine of the priesthood of all believers was one of the major doctrines magnified during the Reformation. It was emphasized in opposition to the prevailing view of the clergy and of the church. The Roman Catholic church held that the layman must approach God through the mediation of a priest. The Reformers insisted that every Christian is a priest and has the right of direct access to God on his own without the necessity of any priestly mediator. The "right of direct access to God" has become a central part of the life of Protestant churches.

However, this is only a fraction of the meaning of this great doctrine. The priesthood of all believers also means that since every Christian is a priest, every Christian also is called to be a minister and has a ministry which must be performed under the judgment of God. This, in turn, means two things. First, *the call to salvation and the call to the ministry is one and the same call.*[5] That is, when one is called by God to be a part of his people, he is also called into the ministry. Young people often struggle with the question as to whether or not they are "called into the ministry." From one perspective, this is a completely irrelevant question. If a person has been called by God to be a Christian, then he has been called into the ministry.

Let us see how this call relates to God's basic call discussed earlier.

God's basic call is a call to mission. This mission is redemptive, and redemption is both personal and social. Every Christian is called to this mission. He fulfills his mission through his ministry. This is his ministry; he cannot evade it; he cannot avoid it; he cannot get someone else to fulfill it for him.

We now have the two answers to our fundamental question: What really does it mean to be the People of God? It is a people called to a mission and called to a ministry. This is what God is about, and this is what he calls us to be about.

This leads us into the second important meaning growing out of God's call to ministry. In the doctrine of the priesthood of all believers and God's call to ministry we find the key to understanding the plan which God ordained to accomplish his redemptive purpose in the world. Namely, he is calling a *people* to be the ministers through whom he may work his work of redemption in the world. Here is the key. This means that *the primary responsibility for God's ministry in the world is the responsibility of the laity and not the clergy*.

The primary responsibility for doing God's work in any given time and place rests upon the shoulders of the congregation—the People of God—rather than upon the church staff. This is a revolutionary concept which the majority simply do not believe and certainly do not practice. Most church members feel that they fulfill their "work for God" when they contribute their money to pay the salary of the clergy, who thus are freed from other work and are able to do the work of God. There are, of course, those who have become aware that they have a responsibility in addition to the giving of money. They teach Sunday school, work with youth groups, visit, etc. But the basic attitude which persists is that the primary responsibility for doing God's work rests upon the shoulders of the clergy.

A hypothetical illustration will prove my point. If, in a given church, attendance at Sunday school begins to decline, if attendance at worship services falls off, if the number of baptisms or church additions decreases significantly, if money for the budget fails to come in, one or two of the most influential members will quietly contact the presiding bishop about his next appointment for the church. Or in those churches that have a congregational polity, the deacons will get together in a secret meeting. The topic for discussion will be, "Maybe we need to change pastors." Why do the elders and the deacons feel that the problem focuses in the pastor? Because, they

Matt 21
Ex 19:5-6

say, "That's *his* job. It's what we called (or hired) him to do. If he can't do it, let's get a man who can." Thus we see the basic attitude of the laity revealed.

I am not trying to defend the ministers. Sometimes churches do need to change pastors. But what I am saying is, here is a tragic misunderstanding concerning the nature of the ministry. In the situation mentioned above, what is needed is not so much a change in ministers but a fundamental change in the congregation. Actually, what happens for God in that place is primarily the responsibility of the laity, the People of God who have been called by God to be ministers in that place. If God's work is not being done, then it is because his ministers, the laity, are failing to carry out their ministry!

What we all need to understand at this point is that this is not a devious plan which a group of scheming preachers worked up to try to trap the laity into doing work which preachers don't want to do. Neither is it a malicious program planned in some denominational headquarters to tap a vast untapped source of manpower. This is God's design for the accomplishing of his redemptive mission in the world, and we have missed it! It is God's plan, and we have been trying some other way. Regardless of what our theology may be theoretically, in actual fact and in practice we have been relying upon the wrong people as ministers for God.

If this is true, obviously it must have a basis in Scripture. In Exodus 19 God was calling a "people" to be for him a "kingdom of priests." He was not calling a special group who alone would have this responsibility. The emphasis is upon all the people and their calling to the ministry. In Matthew 21, again the emphasis is upon the "people"—a "people who would bring forth fruit." In 1 Peter 2:5, 9, we read, "Ye also, as lively stones, are built up a spiritual house, a holy priesthood, to offer up spiritual sacrifices, acceptable to God by Jesus Christ. . . . But ye are a chosen generation, a royal priesthood, a holy nation, a peculiar people; that he should show forth the praises of him who hath called you out of darkness into his marvelous light." (Note the close similarity in these verses and in God's call to the original Israel in Exod. 19:5–6.) Here we find God again calling a people to be his people—a special people. But why? What is the nature of their uniqueness? What is the purpose of their call? God makes this absolutely clear, to "show forth the praises of him who hath called you out of darkness into his marvelous light." They are to be a "holy priesthood." For what purpose? "To offer up spiritual sacrifices, acceptable to God by Jesus Christ."

There are several questions that need to be asked with reference to these verses. First, to whom does the personal pronoun "ye" (or you) refer? It says, "Ye . . . a holy priesthood." "Ye . . . are a royal priesthood, a holy nation, a peculiar people."

To answer this we have to ask, "To whom was this little letter addressed?" We find the answer in 1 Peter 1:1. "Peter, an apostle of Jesus Christ, to the strangers scattered throughout Pontus, Galatia, Cappadocia, Asia, and Bithynia." It was not written simply to bishops or to the clergy. It was written to the scattered Christians. For example, suppose I were to address a letter to "the scattered Christians in New England," or "the scattered Christians in the South," and I were to say to them, "You have been called to be ministers by God. Fulfill your ministry!" Would such a letter refer only to the preachers or to the church staff? Absolutely not! I would be writing primarily to the laity, the People of God. They are the ministers!

This raises a second question. If the layman is the basic minister, what does the text mean when it says he is to "offer spiritual sacrifices"? Earlier it was said that one of the functions of a priest was to serve as a mediator, to seek to bring man and God together. Here we find out that one way in which this function was carried out was by the offering of sacrifices. In the Old Testament one of the functions of a priest was to offer sacrifices to God in behalf of the people. The purposes of these sacrifices were to confess sin, to seek forgiveness, and to bring God and man more closely together. Ultimately the purpose of sacrifices was reconciliation. As members of the people of God, we are called to be priests, and as priests we are to offer "spiritual sacrifices." What does this mean and how do we do it?

A clue to the answer to this question is found in the Book of Hebrews where Jesus is portrayed as the Great High Priest. As the High Priest, Jesus, too, makes sacrifice to God in behalf of the sinful people. He, too, seeks to bring man and God together. Thus the Great High Priest goes into the Holy of Holies to make his sacrifice to God in behalf of the people—and what is the sacrifice he makes? *He offers himself!* He gives his own life!

What is the "sacrifice" which the Christian, as a priest, is to offer to God in behalf of the sinful world? He is to offer himself, his life in ministry! This is precisely what Paul was talking about when he said in Romans 12:1, "I beseech you therefore, brethren, by the mercies of God, that ye present your bodies a living sacrifice, holy, acceptable unto God. . . ."

There is, however, a basic difference in the priesthood of the Old

Testament and the priesthood of the New Testament. In the Old
Testament the priest offered the sacrifice. In the New Testament the
priest *is* the sacrifice! He offers his life to God in behalf of the world
which God is seeking to redeem. This is what it means to be a
minister . . . to be a Christian . . . to be the People of God. It was
God's design and plan from the beginning—and we have missed it!
When God calls a person to be a part of his people, he calls him to
be a minister. The calls are not separate. They are one and the same.

When one truly responds to God, it is to the ministry he is responding. And this ministry is no burden because this is what it means to
"believe" in God. To "believe" in God means to be so caught up with
who God is and with what he is doing in the world that one gives
his life to God to join with him in what he is seeking to do in the
world. This is what makes life thrilling and full of meaning—to be
laborers together with God—because what God is doing in and for
the world is what it so desperately needs! This is something worth
giving one's life to and for. Giving one's life in ministry, ("losing
one's life," as Jesus said, or "offering spiritual sacrifices," according to
1 Peter) is the way to find life—full and abundant.

Still another question needs to be asked. If the laity, the People of
God, are the basic ministers, is there no such thing in the New Testament as the clergy? Yes, there is. What, then, is their task? This is
a fundamental question both for the clergy and for the laity. Many
times the clergy, not understanding clearly their role, have let their
ministry be determined by the places where the pressures were the
greatest. As a result, they have been very unhappy and have found no
fulfillment in the ministry. On the other hand, the laity, through lack
of understanding, have placed responsibilities upon the clergy which
tended to exploit them and did not permit the fulfillment of their
call.

It would be a tremendously releasing experience both for the clergy
and the laity if both came to understand the nature of the specific
"calling" of the clergy. We find the answer to this question in
Ephesians 4:11–12, "And he gave some, apostles; and some, prophets;
and some, evangelists; and some, pastors and teachers; For the per-
fecting of the saints, for the work of the ministry, for the edifying of
the body of Christ." There are three parallel clauses here that seemingly give the functions of the clergy—to perfect the saints, to do the
work of the ministry, and to edify the body of Christ.

We have here what some New Testament scholars call the heresy of the comma. It must be remembered that in the original Greek manuscripts there were no punctuation marks. The way the King James translators punctuated this verse made a very bad translation. Unfortunately the Revised Standard Version is not any better. The best translation, in my judgment, is in the *New English Bible. Good News for Modern Man* is a good translation. If I may be permitted to give a rather free translation, we can see the special task to which the clergy are called. God has called his people, the laity, to be his basic ministers. However, he has called some for special ministry. "He called (appointed) some to be apostles, some to be prophets, some to be evangelists, and some to be pastor-teachers. He called (appointed) these for the purpose of equipping the laity for their ministry, and in this way the body of Christ is to be built up." God has called the laity to be his basic ministers. He has called some to be "player-coaches" (to use Elton Trueblood's term) to equip the laity for the ministry they are to fulfill. This equipping ministry is of unique importance. One is appointed to this ministry by the Holy Spirit, therefore it must be undertaken with utmost seriousness.

This is a radical departure from the traditional understanding of the roles of the laity and the clergy. The laity had the idea that they were already committed to a "full-time" vocation in the secular world, thus they did not have time—at least much time—to do God's work. Therefore they contributed money to "free" the clergy to have the time needed to fulfill God's ministry. This view is rank heresy. If we follow this pattern, we may continue to do God's work until the Lord comes again and never fulfill God's purpose as it ought to be done.

At the present time many people are seeking new ways to prop up sagging organizations. We search for new gimmicks, new promotional schemes, new approaches to make the work of the church more effective. Undoubtedly we do need new approaches. But we will never be effective in doing the work of God until his people whom he has called to be his basic ministers come to understand their call and commit themselves with joyful abandon to fulfilling that call. No organizational approach nor promotional scheme can take the place of this basic need! We have been relying upon the wrong people to do the work of the ministry. God has called his people to be his ministers. His people must understand, accept, become equipped for, and fulfill this call!

2. *The Wrong Place*

Not only have we been relying upon the wrong people, we have been trying to do God's work in the wrong place. What does this mean? We have sought to do the work of God primarily in the church when it must be done primarily in the world. Those of us who are the clergy must confess our sin at this point and accept our share of responsibility for the error in this area. In the past (and for many this continues in the present) when we called upon laymen for ministry, it was almost invariably for a ministry in the church. Many Christians have worked exceedingly hard, but the work they were doing was related primarily to the church as an institution. As a result, we built up the church as an institution until it has become large and relatively rich. But the "world" was left largely untouched. Let me be clear at this point. The layman, in fulfilling his ministry, is not to become a "little preacher." Neither is the ministry of the laity to assist the pastor to do "his" work. (In reality this is not "his" work anyway. The ministry belongs to the laity, not to the clergy. His task is to equip the laity for their ministry.) Neither is the ministry of the laity to "uphold the hands" of the pastor. The layman has a special and unique ministry which only he can perform.[6]

There are two reasons why the ministry of the laity must be primarily in the world. Each of these reasons reveals a fundamental weakness in the present life and work of the church. First, it is in the world where a ministry for God is desperately needed. In the churches we have numerous meetings. We have regular weekly meetings . . . special meetings . . . meetings on Sunday and during the week . . . meetings in the morning and in the evening . . . women's meetings . . . men's meetings. We have large meetings; we have small meetings. And if attendance at some of them begins to decline, we have meetings to find out what's wrong with the attendance at the meetings.

In most of our churches we have no dearth of meetings. What, then, is the weakness in our present approach? We have tried to win the world by holding meetings within our church buildings. There is one tragic flaw in this approach—the "world" does not attend the meetings. The "world" knows little and cares less about what takes place in the meetings we are so careful to hold in our church buildings. Thus, in these meetings we are simply talking to each other. Whether it's a men's meeting or a Bible study class or a meeting of the women, we talk about "loving the world" and "transforming the world," but basically all we do is talk to each other. Then annually (or twice annually) the church has a "special series of services" (a preaching mission or a revival). If it's a Baptist meeting, all the Baptists invite their Methodist, Presbyterian, and Episcopalian friends to attend the services so that the visiting speaker will not be embarrassed by the small attendance. We promise if they will help us out at our meeting, we will help them out when they have theirs. We are masters at self-deception. All the vaunted activity we put into preparation for the special services, all the prayers that were uttered, all the visits that were made, all the effort that was made to "be present every night"—the result is the same—we simply talk to each other. The "world" is untouched. If the world is ever going to be confronted by a ministry for God, it is going to have to be a ministry that is expressed where the world is, namely, in the world.

If the ministry of the laity is to be primarily in the world, we begin to see the wisdom of God's call to the laity to be his basic ministers because it is "in the world" that the laity live. They do not have to make a special visit on Thursday night to get to the world. When Monday morning dawns, they go to the world. They are in the stores, the shops, the offices, the hospitals, the factories, the farms, the homes. The only problem is, being in the world, all they know to do is to "be good." In the main they have no idea how to be a minister for God. There is a vast difference between "being good" and "being a minister." But too many church members have not the slightest idea what this difference is. So the layman must not only be willing to be a minister, he must also learn what it means and learn how to be a minister.

This leads to the second reason why the ministry of the laity must be primarily in the world. The world today insists upon a demonstration of our faith before it will listen to our words. This reveals a second weakness in the life and approach of the present church. We are trying to win the world primarily through the use of words. In classes, in worship services, in special meetings, the church is doing a lot of talking. On the radio and television we talk still more. We bombard the ears of people with words, words, words. However the church is finding it increasingly difficult to get the world to pay any attention to these words. We cry, "Christ Is the Answer." But the world shrugs its shoulders and ignores us. The politicians and men of business make their decisions as though the church did not exist.

Parents are becoming greatly disturbed because the youth are tuning the church out as being irrelevant.

In effect the world is saying to the church, if you people have anything, show it. Don't come quoting Scripture or mouthing words. I want to see a demonstration of what you say. You say that Christ transforms people. You believe that Christ can take a man who in his business is grasping, greedy, and selfish, and transform him and make him into a person who loves people more than money, who is more concerned about the welfare of those in need than he is about grasping and getting more money. You say that Christ can transform people like that? Show me! I don't see this in business where it seems that church people are just as grasping and greedy as the people not in the church. The world says to us, "You speak glibly about the love of God. But if you really want us to understand the love of God, then you be an expression of the love of God. You love us; you care for us; you enter into our lives, our concerns, our hurts as you say God does. Unless you do, your words mean nothing."

If what I am saying is true, then much of what we are now doing in our church programs is exactly backwards. By that I mean that the present church program points toward what happens in the church on Sunday as being the climax. The pastor works all week preparing his sermon. The Bible teachers study for their teaching task. A vigorous effort is made in visitation to get as many people as possible to attend on Sunday. What happens in the church on Sunday—this is the climax!

Oh, no! This is not the climax. The climax is what happens in the world during the week! And yet, in our present church program all our effort is pointed toward trying to get as many as we can to come on Sunday. Don't misunderstand, I am not minimizing what happens on Sunday. This is important, but it is not the climax. Let me illustrate. Here is a church where a thousand people attend services on Sunday. They attend Bible study and enjoy what the teachers have to say, and they listen carefully to what the preacher says in the worship service. It's a good day, they feel. Then Monday comes and they go to their work simply to live their lives as good, decent, respectable people. They come back the following Sunday to repeat the same experience.

Nothing really happens. The world is not touched. On the other hand, consider another church that has only a hundred in attendance on Sunday. But these people are aware that God has called them to a ministry. They know that their ministry is in the world during the week. While in church they study, worship, and open their lives to an infilling by the Spirit of God. However, aware that their ministry is in the world during the week, their eyes are focused on the world. What is the ministry needed? How can they express this ministry? Where is the particular place where the ministry of each one is to be focused? What special plans need to be made? Because of this, what happens in church on Sunday is exceedingly important, but it is not the climax!

When the worship, study, planning, and equipping are completed, they go out to invade the world for God. In stores, shops, offices, factories, homes, farms, each expresses his ministry. Then the next Sunday they return to church. Some are excited because they have experienced a degree of progress in their ministry. Others are bloody because they were "clobbered" by the world. Wounds are bound up. Experiences are shared. Confession is made. Encouragement to try again is given, and new strength is sought from each other and from God. They study again, make more plans, worship and infilling is experienced, prayer is offered. And they go out again. The focus of their attention is always on the world! What happens in the world during the week—this is the climax!

Such being the case, we need to change the basis for evaluating the effectiveness of the work of our churches. At present we tend to evaluate the success of the church on the basis of how many attend on Sunday. Rather, we need to ask, "What did those who attended on Sunday do in the world during the week?" This is what really matters. True, it is not easy to evaluate, but this is where the eyes of the church must be focused.

We need to reevaluate the meetings of our churches. Are the meetings being held really equipping the laity for their ministry in the world? Apparently not, but if the present meetings are not really equipping people for their basic ministry, then we need to change what we are doing and start some that will equip them for their ministry.

What then is God's basic call?

It is a call to mission. A mission that is redemptive in nature. This redemption is personal and social. It is a call to ministry. Each individual is to fulfill God's mission through his own ministry. The call to be a part of God's people and the call to ministry are one and the same.

What does it mean to be the People of God? I think it is a people

who understand the divine mission which God is about in the world
and who believe so deeply in God and what he is doing that they give
their lives to join with him in accompanying this divine redemptive
mission. And wonder of wonders—in doing this these people find life!
Full and abundant life. A free gift from God.

NOTES

1. For a fuller treatment of these issues see Findley B. Edge, *A Quest for
Vitality in Religion* (Nashville: Broadman, 1963), ch. 5–6.

2. Whether this last Hebrew verb is reflexive or not, "bless themselves,"
really does not change the basic meaning.

3. Emil Brunner, *The Word and World* (London: Student Christian
Movement Press, 1931), p. 108.

4. According to Jeremias the early church saw in the parables of Jesus
lessons they applied to their own lives. For technical comments on these
two parables, see Joachim Jeremias, *The Parables of Jesus* (New York:
Charles Scribner's Sons, 1955), pp. 52–64, 70, 76, 100–3. Speaking of Matthew
21: 33–44, Jeremias says, "The parable has become an exact outline of the
story of redemption, from the covenant at Sinai . . . embracing the founding
of the Gentile Church, and passing on to the Last Judgment" (p. 60). Form
critics question whether Jesus ever spoke v. 43.

5. It is true there is a call to a special ministry. The reference here is to
the basic ministry to which every Christian is called.

6. The nature and expression of this ministry are described in ch. 6-8.

CHAPTER THREE

The Nature of God's Mission

The mission of the church is to fulfill God's mission. But in inquiring into the nature of God's mission, and thus asking what should the church be about, we are bringing to the surface one of the most thorny and bristling problems in the life of the present-day church. The issue is emotion-packed. In some instances heated business meetings lasting well past midnight have been held. People have left one church to unite with another. Because of this issue many preachers have left the church ministry. Churches have split, and pastors and staff members have been dismissed. Theological students are agonizing over whether they can or should fulfill their calling in a local church.

The issue is not only difficult, it is complex. Other recent writers have dealt with related aspects of this central issue. It is encouraging that we are coming to see the essential unity of emphases that in the past have been viewed either as polarities or antagonistic. For example, Robert Raines calls attention to the "pietist-secularist" controversy.[1] The pietist, he says, is one who is primarily church-centered. He finds the expression of his religious life in the church and tends to emphasize what God has done in the past, his "mighty acts." On the other hand, the secularist is one who is primarily world-centered. He tends to emphasize what God is doing in the world now, and his major religious expression is service to the world. The pietist is deeply concerned about his own personal spiritual life. The secularist is concerned about the world. The pietist prays, "Lord, change me!" The secularist prays, "Lord, change the world!" Raines points out that both these emphases are necessary. Each provides a necessary corrective to the other. Those who hold to one of these views should not seek to convert the others to their view, but both sides should come to recognize the partiality of their particular position and to incorporate into their thinking the truth in the other view.

Elton Trueblood deals with the same issue but from a slightly different perspective.[2] He uses the terms "pietist" and "activist" to designate the areas of polarity. For him the pietist is the person who magnifies the life of prayer, personal devotion, and individual salvation. Here is an emphasis which is simply indispensable for the dynamic Christian, namely, a consistent, meaningful, personal devotional life. In our day with its emphasis on action, the practice of meditation and devotion has fallen into disrepute. When Bible reading and prayer are observed by Christians, the experience, too often, tends to become dull routine. If the Christian is to have either the desire to minister to the world or anything to share with the world, then his inner life must constantly be refueled by a deep and meaningful devotional life. Many of us through our own experience can attest to the validity of this spiritual truth—there have been times when we experienced aliveness, but there have also been times when because of human frailty we have experienced failure.

On the other hand, according to Trueblood, is the activist whose central word is "involvement." Worship and meditation for him are largely a waste of time. Religion is what a man does. Professions of faith and theological discussions of orthodoxy are totally irrelevant to the present scene and are luxuries that we cannot afford in the modern social crisis. The activist feels that to attack the entrenched social evils is the only adequate way in which to express the Christian life. Both of these emphases historically have been a part of the life of the church. The tragedy of modern churches is that they have become sharply divided over them. The tendency is to take one emphasis or the other and build upon it as though it were the whole truth. And, as Trueblood says, each has an element of truth, but each in denying the validity of the other is denying a part that each needs for its own authenticity. "The polarization of our time . . . produces half men who could be whole men. . . . Service without devotion is rootless; devotion without service is fruitless."[3]

The title of Elizabeth O'Connor's second book, *Journey Inward, Journey Outward,* focuses on the same polarity. Her basic thesis is that one emphasis without the other is completely inadequate. This, she says, "is a book concerned with the renewal of the church, for it holds that renewal cannot come to the church unless its people are on an inward journey. It holds with equal emphasis that renewal cannot come to the church unless its people are on an outward journey."[4] In her emphasis the journey inward involves three "engagements." The first is the engagement with oneself. This means that the Christian must come to have as deep and realistic an understanding of himself as possible. He needs to know the "trigger words" that "set him off" and at what places he is rigid and why. This does not mean that his commitment to the gospel is any less; it simply means that he understands himself better. He understands why he tends to reject some people and accept others, why he feels, thinks, and acts the way he does.

The second engagement is with God. Elizabeth O'Connor points out that although a person cannot really know God without first coming to know himself, yet to know oneself is not to know God. God often speaks through the self but he is more than the self. In this engagement the devotional life is again magnified. Through meditation, prayer, and Scripture the person must "take time to experience a life that is different from his life, and to see a world that is not visible to the ordinary glance."[5] The inward life is the disciplined life. It is neither simple nor easy. There is a price to be paid by the Christian who desires the reality of this life.

The third engagement is with others. These are not the "others" in the world, but "others" in the church. Being "of the household of faith," they are included in the inward journey. This is not a group of like-minded, socially compatible, religious people. These are people with whom we sustain a deep and meaningful relationship. We all confess that "Christ is Lord." Consequently, the church may be composed of a strange assortment, brought together, not by their own selection but by the call of God. This "fellowship of faith" is a strange community where commitment is not tentative. It is a fellowship so real and so deep that we are willing to take risks that would not be taken in other places. It is a risk to know and to be known, to care and to be cared for.

But the inward journey is not enough. There is also the outward journey. The church must take the form of a servant. Elizabeth O'Connor says the ministry of the church is not only to be determined by the areas of need in the community and city in which the church is located; it is determined in part by the gifts of the members discovered in the inward journey.

EVANGELISM AND/OR SOCIAL ACTION

I would like to explore this issue from still a different perspective.

One of the major tragedies of the modern church is its tendency to become polarized around either evangelism or social action. One group tends to place its sole emphasis on the necessity for personal salvation. The other group tends to emphasize the necessity of social involvement. This polarity has its roots far back in Christian history. However, it is of special significance today because it is the issue that is causing deep divisions in denominations; it is causing splits in churches; it is causing some to leave the church. But the major significance concerning this polarity is that it raises the question concerning the basic nature of the gospel. I believe that the gospel demands an emphasis on both evangelism and social action. The church that neglects either emphasis demonstrates a serious misunderstanding as to the nature of the gospel.

To put this issue in proper context we return to the questions which introduced this chapter. What is the nature of the church? If the church is a witnessing community instead of simply a company of believers, what is the nature of the witness it is to give? If the church is mission, what is the nature of its mission? If the mission of the church is to fulfill God's mission, what is the nature of God's mission in the world? If God's mission is to bring reconciliation to man, what is involved in this reconciliation? If man needs reconciliation, what does this say about his nature and his need? The answers the church gives to these difficult theological questions determine her life and ministry.

To put the issue in still sharper focus, it is necessary to use some theological "labels." This is unfortunate because so often labels carry emotional overtones. Such is not intended here. I use these labels simply to designate a general theological position.

There are those who are called "fundamentalists." This group has a certain doctrine of God, a certain doctrine of man, and a certain doctrine of salvation. They hold that man is a "fallen creature," a sinner, alienated from God. This means that man is "lost" and doomed for eternity. The only way man can be saved is through a personal experience with Christ or by entering into a "saving relationship" with Christ. They demonstrate a deep zeal in seeking to lead man out of his "lost" condition into a "saving relationship" by holding revival meetings, passing out tracts, visiting in homes, and holding prayer meetings. In numerous and various ways they seek to lead "lost" man to be saved. Though undoubtedly there are sociological factors involved, something of the depth and effectiveness of their zealous concern is demonstrated by the fact that these are the churches that are growing most rapidly at the present time while most of the others are declining.

However, some of us believe that their views of God, man, and salvation are too narrow. The emphasis is on the vertical relationship—man's relationship with God—but the horizontal relationship—man's relationship with his fellow-man—is either under-played or ignored. Man is not just a "soul"; he is a unity, a human being, and salvation is not only concerned with what takes place in the life after death but also with life here and now. God is concerned about the totality of the life of his children and this includes their human, social situation. Therefore, we reject this theology because it is too limited.

On the other hand there is the group who are called "liberals." They, too, have a doctrine of God, man, and salvation. Among these people a deep concern for man in terms of his social needs is demonstrated. They dare to become involved in the lives of others, often at great personal sacrifice and at great personal risk. William String-fellow, a lawyer and brilliant lay-theologian, is a rugged example of this kind of concern and involvement. Listen to him.

> This was to be home. It had been home before: for a family of eight —five kids, three adults. Some of their belongings had been left behind. Some of their life had, too.
> The place, altogether, was about 25 x 12 feet, with a wall separating the kitchen section from the rest. In the kitchen was a bathtub, a tiny, rusty sink, a refrigerator that didn't work, and an ancient gas range. In one corner was a toilet with a bowl without a seat. Water dripped perpetually from the box above the bowl. The other room was filled with beds; two double-decker military cots, and a big ugly convertible sofa. There wasn't room for anything else. The walls and ceilings were mostly holes and patches and peeling paint, sheltering legions of cockroaches.
> This was to be my home.
> I wondered, for a moment, why.
> Then I remembered that this is the sort of place in which most people live, in most of the world, for most of the time. This or something worse.
> Then I was home.
> It was to Harlem that I came from the Harvard Law School. I came to Harlem to live, to work there as a lawyer, to take some part in the politics of the neighborhood, to be a layman in the church there.
> It is now seven years later.[6]

Here is commitment to involvement that is quite astounding. As a graduate of Harvard Law School, he could have had a nice position in a variety of law firms in New York. Instead he chose to live with, to identify with (at considerable personal risk), the alienated, the rejected, the hopeless. There have been many in less dramatic ways who have dared to demonstrate their concern and involvement. They seek better schools, work for integration, agitate for better housing, thus saying, "You are not forgotten; we care."

But liberal theology is too narrow. Its emphasis is on the horizontal relationship, and the vertical relationship is neglected. Man must not only be rightly related to his fellow-man, he must be rightly related to God. Granted that man has certain human needs that must be met, he also has spiritual needs that must be met. Man's basic problem is sin and his fundamental need is salvation, and this need is met only by coming to know God in a personal relationship. To provide better housing, education, wages, as fine as these are, still leaves man's spiritual needs untouched.

Personally, I identify myself in a group somewhere between these two extremes. This group cuts across all denominational lines. It has a doctrine of God, man, and salvation. There is recognition of the necessity for an emphasis on both the vertical and horizontal relationships—man must be rightly related both to God and to his fellow-man. We recognize that man is a sinner and alienated from God, and the only way man can come into a right relationship with God is through a personal experience with Jesus Christ, but at the same time, we believe that man is a human being with needs. God is concerned with the total life of his creatures, and therefore we must be deeply concerned about man in the totality of his social needs.

Although this group holds to a sound theology and an adequate social concern, there is a serious and tragic weakness. *We demonstrate neither the zeal of the Fundamentalist nor the involvement of the Liberal!* We may hold a "better" theology, but our "correct" theology is worthless unless it makes us *do* something. In fact our "correct" theology is a judgment upon us unless we act upon it. The plea here is that the church come to recognize and demonstrate with boldness both personal salvation and social concern. This is what the gospel demands. Anything other than this, anything less than this, is a tragic perversion of the gospel. Let us now examine the reasons, in light of the gospel, why both of these emphases must be sought after with equal zeal and why either emphasis alone is most inadequate.

INADEQUACY OF SOCIAL EMPHASIS ALONE

In reaction against the social gospel movement of the first part of this century, many churches turned to a strong evangelical emphasis in their ministry. The atrocities and other events attending the Second World War exploded the "rosy" view of man that had previously been held. The crisis theology from Europe came to give a theological base for a different view of man. Evidently in order to make sure that the "social issue" did not confuse the church as to what her basic task was, any serious social concern was practically eliminated from the ministry of the church.

In the last several decades the almost exclusive emphasis in many churches has been on the personal and evangelistic aspects. Thus it is only natural that the recent "new stirrings" in religion should focus on what were seen to be major weaknesses in the life of the church. One of these weaknesses was a lack of serious social concern and involvement. Also numerous other factors in our society were beginning to focus attention on the social plight of the alienated in society. When the renewal movement began to take shape in the mid-fifties and early sixties, a major emphasis was placed on social concern and social involvement because this was what was missing in the life of the church. We began to hear words and phrases like, "the servant church," "where the action is," "let the world write the agenda," "a man for others," etc.

Some churches began to express this social concern in a radical form. In ministering to hippies, drug users, and the alienated, churches attempted to "meet the world on the world's terms." In many instances churches were careful not to speak any "religious word" because they did not want to give the impression that they were trying to "impose religion" on these people. So great was this emphasis on social concern that in some circles the "renewal movement" has come to be viewed as a "neo-social gospel" movement. This tendency to identify "renewal" with "social action" has caused some to reject the whole idea of renewal, and this is tragic because the church stands in desperate need of renewing. Those who have magnified the need for social concern and social involvement have made a most significant contribution to the life of the total church, because this was the raw nerve that needed to be touched and exposed. However, in light of the total gospel, they have been grossly in error in letting social concern become their only emphasis. But let's be specific.

1. *"Become more human"*

Every new movement tends to develop its own jargon. The renewal

movement is no exception. One of the "in" phrases which writers
have used with frequency is "more human." They say that the purpose
of the gospel or the task of the church is to help people become "more
human."

What is meant by this phrase? Those who use it seem to indicate
by their attitude that its meaning is quite clear and that one ought
to be able to understand it without difficulty. Yet I have searched in
vain for anyone who gives a satisfactory explanation as to its meaning.

I must confess I am disturbed by the use of the phrase, "Be more
fully human." Is this simply another instance of a semantic problem?
Or is it a subtle (or not so subtle) shift in theology? If those who
use the phrase mean "helping people to fulfill the humanity God
intended in creation," then I can agree with it. But if they mean that
man is essentially good and that he simply needs to fulfill his own
innate potential and that this can be done in his own strength, this
implies a theological view of man that needs to be seriously challenged.

Man does need to become "more human" in terms of his original
creation. He does need to fulfill his potential. But another question
needs to be raised. How does a person become "what God intended
him to be"? Is this accomplished by helping the individual work
through all his psychological hang-ups, by helping him to have an
adequate income and adequate housing? That a person needs these
things is without question. But when a person has these "things," has
he become "what God intended"? Is this all that man needs? My
answer is, No!

Fundamental here, of course, is one's doctrine of man. What is the
nature of man, and what is his need? If the advocates of "helping
people become more fully human" mean that they want to take what
is in man and develop more of the same, this is inadequate. Human
nature is not in order but in disorder. Therefore, from one perspective,
to "become more fully human" is to become more disordered. How is
the human predicament to be met?

The fundamental disorder in man is met by the individual having
an encounter with Christ in which he becomes a "new creature." According to Paul this comes only by being "in Christ." What man needs
in terms of his basic nature is not "more of the same" but a "new
nature." The Bible does not speak about becoming "more human"
but about a "new humanity." In terms of the nature and the needs
of man the Bible speaks of a "new creation" (2 Cor. 5:17).

Our age is enamored of slogans. One of the most popular has been, "You are a soul brother." A fellow minister pointed out to me that the emphasis in this slogan needs to be changed. He said what we really need to say to people is, "You are a soul, brother!"[7] You are more than education, more than housing, more than wages. You are these things, certainly, and these need to be cared for. But you are more! You are a soul, brother. If you would be completely human, if you would know life in its wholeness, then you must come to know God as he is revealed in Jesus Christ.

This does not mean that we do not accept a person as he is, where he is. Certainly, in relating to a person, in spite of the sin and distortions of his life, we care for him. We accept him as he is. In loving and accepting him I do not have to close my eyes to reality and act as though nothing was wrong. When a physician examines a patient and finds a potentially deadly disease, he doesn't try to relate to the patient by saying, "You are fine." The kindest, most loving, most caring thing he can do is to tell the patient exactly the seriousness of his disease and what can be done to cure it.

In relating realistically to a brother, I confess that I have "not arrived." I am a fellow struggler . . . one who is "on the way." But I do feel that in the midst of this existence I have found "The Way" and him who gives meaning to this existence as well as direction and strength for living it.

Being accepted is important, but man desperately needs something more than acceptance. With keen insight Professor William Muehl of Yale Divinity School expresses his frustration at all the talk about "being accepted." He says the idea that one "has been 'accepted' by God is one of the worst bits of bad news ever to issue from the murky caverns of Teutonic theology." Basically man wants and needs not to be accepted but to be loved, and there is a tremendous difference between the two.

To say that a man is "accepted" as though there were no meaning in the universe, as though there were no goal, no standards, no judgment is totally unrealistic. "To be loved gives man a sense of personal significance. Because in spite of all the nonsense spoken by theologians and psychotherapists, love is both demanding and judging."[8] Love is neither blind nor unrealistic. Love knows you as you are and loves you as you are. But love also knows what you can be and yearns for you to become this. Because there is meaning in the universe and because there is purpose for life, love suffers when this meaning and purpose are missed. "A God who loves men, specific men, actual combinations of virtues and vices, with a love which reflects and responds to variable qualities in each one of them gives meaning to life and dignity to history. But a God who 'accepts' us without regard to these attributes which distinguish one character and caliber from another destroys the whole concept of human personality. So, Brother, be of good cheer. You are *not* accepted. You are loved. And what is equally important, you still have the freedom to reject that love and go to Hell!"[9]

God is holiness and justice as well as love. His very being could not ignore or condone man's sinfulness. It is a demonstration of his great love that he went to such limits to make possible man's "acceptance." But God's acceptance is not at the expense of violating either God's nature or man's freedom.

I, too, believe in helping people become "whole." I believe in ministering to the "total man." But this can be done only by ministering to man in terms of his spiritual needs as well as in terms of his human needs. Those humanitarians who are concerned about man in his human needs and who minister to him in these areas do a good thing. Their weakness, however, is that they fail in their primary task; namely, they fail to minister to the total man and to help him to become "whole."

2. *Universal Salvation*

There is another group that tends to major on ministering to man in terms of his social needs. They hold the view of universal salvation. Their position is that all men are either already saved or will be sometime in the future. Theirs is not a "rosy" view of man which emphasizes man's essential goodness as would tend to be the view of the position discussed above. Rather they speak positively and convincingly of "the fact of man's sin" and that he is a sinner. They recognize the "factor of degeneracy" within man "and of sin as its cause."[10] But this same writer in another place says that God is not only "seeking to reconcile every individual to Himself, but also that He will in the end succeed in so doing. For only on that basis can we speak of the ultimate victory of a God who is love. To a God who is primarily justice an irreconcilable sinner dispatched to everlasting damnation, or even eliminated altogether, might be a triumph, but to a God who is primarily love it could only be the most absolute form

of defeat. Thus the profound concern of religious faith for God's ultimate victory seems, in its Christian form, to move unavoidably to-
wards universalism [universal salvation]."[11]

If the concept of universal salvation is correct, then it is easily understandable why those holding this view would place their emphasis
primarily, if not exclusively, upon ministering to man in the area of
his social needs. If man is either already saved (though he may not
know it), or if he is going to be saved sometime in the future on the
basis of God's irresistible wooing, and this outcome is set regardless of
what he does, this certainly takes away from the area of Christian
witness the deep sense of urgency concerning the destiny of man. Of
course, those who hold this view would say that it is better "in this
life" for man to be made aware that he is already "saved." But the
sense of urgency that comes when a person's eternal destiny hangs in
the balance is certainly lost. Thus, in practice, the major thrust is to
minister to man in his social needs. The "spiritual" dimension is
either minimized, neglected, or lost.

It is now necessary to inquire (though altogether too briefly)
whether this view of universal salvation has a solid foundation in Holy
Scriptures.[12] The basic thesis of those who accept the concept of universal salvation is that the eternal redemptive purpose of God for
man will not and cannot be thwarted. Actually from a biblical perspective this view does not have particularly strong support. As one
writer says, in "the Bible there are hints and hopes of universal salvation."[13] In the teachings of Jesus we would have to strain at an
interpretation to find support for this position. The parable of the
rich man and Lazarus (Luke 16:19-31) is sometimes cited. It is
pointed out that the rich man's experience in hell was already beginning to work a regenerative work upon him—he was becoming
concerned about his brothers. Or, in the parable of the prodigal son,
attention is called to the fact that when the son returned he was
greeted by his father not with the words, "You are a sinner," but
with the gracious words, "This my son" (Luke 15:24). Again, in the
same chapter, the shepherd seeks the lost sheep "until he finds it"
(Luke 15:4). And the woman seeks the lost coin "until she finds it"
(Luke 15:8). In John 12:32 Jesus states, "And I, if I be lifted up
from the earth, will draw all men unto me." Again, from the lips of
Jesus, "God sent not his Son into the world to condemn the world;
but that the world through him might be saved" (John 3:17).

To deduce the concept of universal salvation from these teachings

of Jesus we would have to go against the more obvious and logical
interpretations of these passages. It might be pointed out that the rich
man in the parable, before expressing this so-called "concern for his
brothers," first asked for water for himself. But more important is the
nature of the interpretation of a parable. A parable, as a rule, teaches
one major truth. Every detail is not expected to carry equal weight. To
base a doctrine on an incidental statement in a parable is indeed a
precarious procedure to follow. The prodigal's father did say, "This my
son." But if we read the whole sentence, the father says, "This my son
was dead . . . this my son was lost." Which means that before the son's
repentance he was alienated, lost, and dead. The "until he finds it"
in the parables of the sheep and coin indicates God's serious per-
sistence in seeking his own. This is not a detail intended to teach a
doctrine. Jesus' statement that his purpose was not "to condemn the
world" but rather that the world "might be saved," indicates God's
intention, not an accomplished fact. In the very next verse Jesus goes
on to say, "He who believes in him is not condemned; he who does
not believe is condemned already" (John 3:18, RSV).

The universalists find a bit more firm ground in some of Paul's
writings. They cite such passages as the following. "God was in Christ
reconciling the world to himself" (2 Cor. 5:19, RSV). "Therefore, as
by the offense of one judgment came upon all men to condemnation;
even so by the righteousness of one the free gift came upon all men
unto justification of life" (Rom. 5:18). "Wherefore God also hath
highly exalted him, and given him a name which is above every
name: That at the name of Jesus every knee should bow, of things
in heaven, and things in earth, and things under the earth; and that
every tongue should confess that Jesus Christ is Lord, to the glory of
God the Father" (Phil. 2:9-11). "For as in Adam all die, even so in
Christ shall all be made alive. . . . For he must reign, till he hath put
all enemies under his feet" (1 Cor. 15:22, 25). Their interpretation
is that God's mighty act in Christ has already accomplished salvation
for every man. They view reconciliation for every man as an accomplished fact. In Christ's act, "all shall be made alive." The enemies
of sin and death have already been defeated for every man.

The error of this interpretation is that it treats as an accomplished
fact that which is God's intention. It is clearly God's intention that
every man be saved. "Not willing that any should perish, but that all
should come to repentance" (2 Pet. 3:9). God's mighty act in Christ
makes salvation for every man a *possibility*. But whether this salva-

tion, which is a possibility, becomes an actuality depends clearly upon man's response. "As many as received him, to them gave he power to become the sons of God" (John 1:12). Although there are a few other passages that the universalists cite, the same objection and response could be made. The biblical base for this position is not well founded.

Actually the view of universal salvation is based more on philosophical theology than on biblical theology. That is, from a philosophical perspective those who hold this view have difficulty with the position that any man's final destiny could be separation from God. Thus, coming to a contrary view, they seek justification from the Scriptures for their position. Their position rests primarily on two aspects of the nature of God, namely, the love of God and the power of God. They hold that if God is a God of infinite love, it is inconceivable that he would ever create a situation in which any whom he loved could suffer ultimate alienation from him. Thus any kind of final destiny in which it is possible for man to be separated from God is a contradiction to the nature of a God who is infinite love.

The concept of a God who is all-powerful is equally threatened, they contend. If it is God's intent that all should be saved (as the Scriptures indicate), then for God not to be able to bring this to pass means that he is less than all-powerful. If God is sovereign power then his purposes cannot be thwarted. If, on the other hand, his purposes can be thwarted, then God is less than almighty. Their logic is simple and seemingly airtight. Concerning man's ultimate salvation either God can or he can't. Either he will or he won't. If God can save all men, but he won't, God is less than infinite love. If God wills that all be saved, but he can't, then God is less than all-powerful. But God is infinite love and all-powerful, therefore he can and will save all men.

The advocates of this view differ as to how and when this universal salvation has or will take place. There are those who hold that man's salvation was accomplished in God's action in the crucifixion. The "good news" of the gospel that man needs to hear is, "You are saved!" The "good news" is not that it is possible for man to be saved; the "good news" is that man has already been saved. Man does not need to accept salvation; he simply needs to recognize that he already has received salvation. Others disagree with this view, evidently feeling that it is too mechanical in nature and does not adequately take into account man's freedom. They feel that man's freedom makes it imperative that he have a choice in his salvation. However they believe

that God's love is ultimately going to be so irresistible that every man
will *have* to choose salvation. God's irresistible quest for man not only
takes place in this life but it carries over in the life to come. Even hell
itself will be used by God as an instrument of causing men to "choose
God." What the proponents of this view fail to recognize is that they
simply push back the problem of freedom one step. If God's quest
after man is "irresistible" so that he "has" to choose God, then man
is no longer free.

From a human perspective this view is exceedingly attractive and
certainly has a deep emotional pull to it. Any sensitive person would
like to feel that this existence of ours is going to have a "story book"
ending. The "good guys" are going to overcome the "bad guys." In
fact, all the "bad guys" are going to become "good guys" and all ultimately are going to be saved. Who would not rejoice if this were
the end result of our existence? However, we have to inquire whether
this view is consistent with reality as we know it in God and in ourselves.

To respond to the advocates of universal salvation on their own
terms, namely, from the perspective of philosophical theology, it must
be pointed out that this position is vulnerable at two strategic points—
the nature of love and the nature of man's freedom.[14] The nature of
love must be examined both from the perspective of God, the lover,
and from the response of man, the loved. First, it must be noted that
the very essence of the nature of love is that it is not coercive; it is
voluntary. Love does not, and cannot, force its way into a life without the person's consent. A love that is described as some kind of
"force" coming to engulf man with irreversible certainty is less than
even the love with which most of us are familiar on the human level.
It is certainly less than the expression of the love of God as revealed
in Jesus. Love can do many things. It can woo; it can allure; it can
plead; it can weep. But the moment it seeks to coerce, love ceases to
be, and something of a different nature comes into being. "Irresistible
love" is a contradiction in terms. When a force becomes irresistible
it is something other than love.

Man's response, as the loved, must also be voluntary. Just as love
cannot force its way into the life of another, neither can a loving response be *forced* (irresistible) from the one loved. A response freely
and voluntarily given is the very essence of love. An external force
may elicit a certain type of response. Force can secure conformity.
But a *loving* response cannot be forced. A loving response is one that

is *given* from within a person, by the person. It is not a response that is forced from without. Thus the position of universalism is weak at one of the central points where it is supposed to be strong—in magnifying the love of God. The kind of irresistible love the universalists advocate contradicts the very nature of love itself.

The second major weakness of the universalists' position involves their view of God's sovereign power and man's freedom. They contend that God's power is absolute and by this they mean that God is able to do anything he desires to do. Since the Scriptures state that it is God's desire that "none should perish" but that all should be saved, and since God is able to do anything he desires, then the inevitable outcome is that all will be saved. For God to have as his eternal purpose that all should be saved, and for this not to take place could mean only one thing—God was not able to "bring it off." This in turn means that God is not all-powerful.

How shall we respond to this contention? This position, in tending to make God's power absolute, has an inadequate view of man's freedom. Freedom is the very essence of man's uniqueness as a human being. An animal such as a horse or a dog is not human because it has no freedom to make any choice in the area of destiny. But man, as a human animal, does have this freedom. If this freedom is in any way limited or taken away from man, then he really becomes no more than any other "dumb" animal. On the other hand, if this freedom is real, then he must have the freedom to thwart even the purpose of God.

How is this concept of man's freedom to be harmonized with the view of God's power? The One who is all-powerful has the power to limit his power. When God created man and gave him freedom and thus made him a "human" being rather than a "mechanistic" being, he placed a very real limitation upon himself. This was God's intent; this was God's design. God had the "power" to do it differently had he so desired. It was a *free* human being, not a robot, with whom God desired fellowship in creation. God takes man's freedom with utmost seriousness. He will not violate it.

The advocates of universal salvation seek to get around this problem in two ways. They say that God in his sovereign power controls man's freedom for man's own good. This argument is relatively weak because it seems to imply that man's freedom is an illusion and not real. It seems to imply that God gives man freedom in areas that are not crucial, but when he gets to the crucial issue of his destiny, then

God withdraws man's freedom and takes over in determining his destiny.

A much stronger argument is that God does take man's freedom with complete seriousness and that man himself makes his own choice determining his destiny. However, the universalist says that God's persuasion will be of such nature that man will inevitably, at some time, choose Him. This "persuasion" which God exercises may be both positive and negative; it can be wooing or punitive. In seeking man, God can make his way so attractive, so alluring, so desirable, so "right" that man simply cannot resist. Man has freedom and he chooses. The choice is not forced. Man is so overwhelmed with the truth of God's way and the rightness of God's way, that he simply cannot resist.

It is easy to recognize some validity in such an argument. God does come to man in wooing winsomeness. God does persuade by the truth and rightness of his way. Man, facing this truth, in freedom may choose God's way. But when one says *all* men *must* inevitably choose God's way, a whole new factor is introduced into the picture. Here is a determinism that is inconsistent with man's freedom.

God's persuasion to accomplish his eternal purpose may also be negative or punitive. This is how Nels Ferré views hell. In his position Ferré seeks diligently to give a large place to man's freedom. In his freedom man may die and go to hell. At some time (in hell) man will have to face his sin. It will not be glossed over; man will have to repent of his sin and be forgiven. He will also have to pay the penalty for his sin. However, the horrors of hell, whatever these may be, and the sufferings endured in hell, whatever these are, will be such that at some time man will come to see the error of his way and will choose God's way. He makes his own choice. But such pressure will be brought to bear on the individual that ultimately he will come to make the right decision. To use Ferré's words, God will "put the screws on hard enough to make men want to change their ways."[15]

Again this is not an adequate solution to the problem of man's freedom. The problem, instead of being solved, is simply pushed back into life after death. In spite of the insistence that man is free and makes his own choice, in spite of whether persuasion or pressure is used, when one says what the final outcome *must be* and what *all men* must do, then really there is no way for man to do otherwise. Man is not free. In spite of all efforts to the contrary, the vaunted talk about man's freedom is empty words. Without freedom life becomes a farce. It is a game that is played, full of sound and fury, persuasion and pressure, but in the end really signifying nothing.

An amazing thing has happened. Those who set out in their goal to help man to "become more fully human," in their solution, have ended up making him less human. They have taken away man's freedom. Sensitivity, emotion, and philosophical logic make universal salvation a highly desirable view of human destiny. But it is a solution purchased at too high a price—the price of human freedom. Thus we must conclude that all will not automatically be saved. Therefore the necessity of each person having a personal encounter with God through Christ and making a personal choice is an absolute essential.

3. *The Christian Presence*

There is a third inadequate view that needs brief consideration. This view places its emphasis on the manner in which the church gives its witness rather than on theology. In the end, however, a theological perspective becomes a central issue. The advocates of this view are concerned with the area of human need and with being "where the action is." They speak of "being there." While "there," the Christian is to express genuine love and concern for individuals and groups. He is to meet them, care for them, and minister to them at the point of their need. He is also to work against whatever it is that alienates and exploits by changing the structures of society.

This position is generally referred to as "the Christian Presence." Historically it came into being just after the Second World War with the Catholic "worker-priest" approach. Theologically, it finds a part of its base in the nature of God. Its exponents say that the basic designation for God, "I am that I am," may be understood as "I am he who is present." A second base is found in the Incarnation. God, throughout the Old Testament period, sought to reveal himself to man in a variety of ways. Always this self-disclosure was inadequate and limited. His supreme self-disclosure was in the person of his son. "God, who at sundry times and in divers manners spake in time past unto the fathers by the prophets, Hath in these last days spoken unto us by his Son" (Heb. 1:1-2). That which previously had been "Word" became "flesh, and dwelt among us" (John 1:14). This was God's supreme act of "being present" in the world. The fullness of God's nature was revealed by the loving care and concern for persons demonstrated by Jesus, the Living Presence in the world.

All who emphasize the necessity for a Christian presence do not mean the same thing when they use the term. There are at least four possible meanings which might be identified.

(1) To be present and to speak an evangelical word when and if appropriate. Believers in this concept have deep and genuine sensitivity to man in his social need and seek to "be present" to man in these needs. However, they feel that man has a spiritual need which can be met only by a personal and continuing relationship with Jesus Christ. Therefore, at some time in their "being present" to an individual, a relationship will be built up in such fashion that they will have an opportunity to speak the word that will point the person to Christ. And he meets man at all points of his need.

(2) To be present and to speak. There is a deep and genuine sensitivity to man in his social need among this group. However, the word they speak—when a word is spoken—is, "You have been saved! Rejoice!" This is the position of those who hold the view of universal salvation discussed above.

(3) To be present and to be silent. Like the other two, holders of this view take with utmost seriousness man in his social need. Because of their theology they are really not concerned about speaking any "word" to man. No verbal expression is needed. The deed itself carries whatever "message" is needed.

(4) To be present to the structures of society. This group might speak of "evangelism," but to them evangelism is "redeeming" the structures of society. It is not personal but social.

This emphasis on "being present" came as a reaction to several weaknesses in the life of the church today. It was a reaction to the tendency of the church to separate religion and life. Religion came to be "something done in church." It was a matter of being "born into the church" and participating occasionally in some sacraments. Or it became a matter of "believing certain doctrines" and attending some meetings. But those who advocated involvement saw that this was an inadequate expression of religion. They insisted that religion must be related to this life with its joys and sorrows, with its hopes and fears, with its victories and defeats.

The "being present" emphasis was also a reaction to the excessive verbalism by which the church expressed its witness to people. The church has tended to rely almost exclusively upon words as the method by which it informed men of God's love and care for them. Whether the witness was through proclamation from a pulpit, or in some massive revival meeting, or on a person-to-person basis, the method of witness was through words. But the advocates of "presence" ask, how can a person understand the words, "God loves you," when all his life he has known nothing but hatred and rejection? Before he can even begin to understand the word "love" he must experience love. This is what Christian presence seeks to do.

Finally, it is a reaction against an expression of religion that is concerned only, or even primarily, with the saving of a "soul" and with life after death. These people say that the church has failed tragically to demonstrate any adequate concern for man in the totality of his life and in the here and now. It is this they seek to express through Christian presence.

Thus with their concern for man and in their desire to become genuinely involved in man's plight they speak of "being open to the world." Another widely acclaimed slogan is, "Let the world write the agenda." An effort is made to discover "new shapes of missionary obedience." Great emphasis is placed on secularity. There is concern for the "secular city," a desire to minister to "secular man" through "secular evangelism."

What should be said concerning this emphasis? This concern for man in the totality of life is certainly good. It is a needed antidote to a traditional emphasis that concentrated primarily on a person's "soul" and with the "hereafter." However, this emphasis falls prey to a serious error. As so often happens, in calling attention to an area of serious neglect, its advocates have emphasized an essential part as though it were the whole. They neglect the other essential: the personal element both in religion and in the life of man. With their emphasis on changing the social structures they, in reality, dehumanize people. While there is a concern for man, it is for man in the masses. They fail to show adequate concern for him as an individual, and they dehumanize him by treating him as a statistic. They want to eliminate ghettos and get better housing for one hundred thousand people, and this is highly desirable as far as it goes. But the individual in this mass with all of his personal problems and needs, his hurts and hopes, his despair and dreams is frequently ignored. Along with the need of society to be made new, the individual human being needs to be loved, cared for, and made new. The latter does not flow automatically from the former.

There is another view held by the "Christian Presence" advocates that needs to be faced and answered. They believe that those who emphasize the necessity of personal salvation demonstrate a prideful arrogance in saying they "have something" which "the world" does not have. There is the feeling that traditional evangelism suggests a "certainty of faith and purpose" which is offensive to some and difficult to accept by others. They shrink from the seeming certainty of the one who says, "I am saved" (or "I am being saved").

True, there could be danger here and some may have given the impression of arrogance. This is unfortunate. But there is also a tragic danger on the other side into which the advocates of "Christian Presence" seem to have fallen. It is possible to say, "I am saved," completely without arrogance because this salvation is not one's own doing, it is a gift. The Christian can freely admit to a fellow struggler that in his own life he has "not arrived." But to say this does not mean that he has not begun this trek with Christ. As Paul says, "I count not myself to have apprehended: but . . . I press toward the mark . . ." (Phil. 3:13–14). Perhaps we have had our fill of an arrogant religion that did not identify adequately with the world. But in seeking to identify with the world let us not lose our identity with God. Because I don't know everything about God does not mean that I know nothing about him.

The Christian can, indeed he must, confess to his fellow-man that in his daily walk he is not perfect. He is a sinner. But because he has to confess to his friend that "I am not what I ought to be" does not mean that he cannot give a joyful witness to the truth that "I am not what I used to be." We must identify with people in their humanity, their sin, and their frailty because that's where we are too. But because of who God is, because of what Christ has done for the world, and more specifically what Christ has done and is doing in our personal lives, we have a witness to proclaim! The revolutionaries who change and transform the world are never unsure of their message nor unclear as to their goal! They are revolutionary precisely because they have a witness which the world doesn't have but which, they think, it desperately needs!

THE NECESSITY FOR AN EVANGELICAL[16] EMPHASIS

With our growing concern for meeting man in his social needs, is there an equal imperative for an emphasis on personal evangelism? It is pointed out by those who hold the view of "Christian Presence" that Jesus was an incarnate witness. His life was a living demonstration of his message. This is true, but it must also be remembered that along with being a "Presence," Jesus also spoke. He interpreted the mean-

ing of "Presence," and what he said was, "The Son of man is come
to seek and to save that which was lost" (Luke 19:10).

There are two major issues that are foundational in our present
inquiry. First, what is the nature of man, and thus what is man's basic
need? Second, what is the nature of salvation, and how is man's need
met?

1. *The Fact of Sin*

What is the nature of human nature? How serious is man's problem? Is it such that he can deal with it in his own strength? The witness of the Bible is that man is a sinner. "For all have sinned, and
come short of the glory of God" (Rom. 3:23). This sin is not minor
wrongdoings. It is of a most serious nature, reaching to the very center of our being and because of it we are "by nature the children of
wrath" (Eph. 2:3). Because of sin man is alienated from God and
"the wages of sin is death" (Rom. 6:23).

There is a tendency on the part of some religious thinkers to minimize the fact of sin. They sometimes refuse to use the term, or when
they do they use it only most reluctantly, preferring rather to speak of
"mistakes," "maladjustments," "societal gaps," etc. This is a far cry
from the biblical view of man. In the Bible there is none of Rousseau's
optimism about the nature of man. There is no humanistic doctrine
of man's innate self-sufficiency. The Bible treats the human predicament with utmost seriousness. Sin is personal. Sin is against God. Man
is responsible. As George Forrell says, "All man's troubles stem from
this one source. None can be solved ultimately unless the relationship
to God, broken through sin, is restored."[17]

There is not order but disorder at the center of man's life. Certainly we need to help change a person's environment. Certainly we
need to help provide for him the best social, economic, and emotional
setting possible in which to live. But doing this will not solve *all* his
problems. Man has problems within—of a specifically personal and
spiritual nature—which must be met.

A few years ago I was visiting in New York City. Because of my
deep concern to find ways of bridging the gap between church and
world, I went to visit and to make a brief study of one of the widely
known churches there that had a reputation for bridging this gap.
After interviewing members of the church staff and getting all the in-

formation and materials I could, one of the staff members suggested
that perhaps I would like to interview some of the members and get
the picture from their perspective. I jumped at the opportunity. He
gave me the names and addresses of several members and made calls
to set up these visits. One of these was a black lady, seemingly in her
mid-thirties, who lived in one of the high-rise apartments nearby. She
was married and had seven children, but her husband was dead. The
difficulty of her struggle was obvious, but her apartment was neat and
clean and from all outward appearances she had everything "under
control." I introduced myself and stated the purpose of my visit, ex-
plaining that I was interested in her church because it was one of the
few that was seriously seeking to express a social concern for people.
We talked for some time about the church, the world, and the problems people face. Suddenly, as if she could contain it no longer, she
exploded, "The church has lied to us!"

I was shocked by the outburst, but, trying to appear casual,
I asked, "What do you mean, 'The church has lied to you'?" Her
reply was, "The church told us that our problem was poor housing.
The church told us that our problem was lack of education and of
adequate wages. It is true that we do need better housing, better
education and better wages. But," she said, "these are not our basic
problems. Our basic problem is within us. These other problems can
be solved. We could get better housing, education, and wages, but
this would not remedy our condition because our basic problem would
still be with us. The church hasn't told us this! And that's why I say
the church has lied to us."

I do not want to imply that I am citing this lady as an authorita-
tive theologian. Here, however, was a person who was exposed to the
social emphasis in religion but who had come to see that it failed to
meet her need. Out of her existential situation, her experience confirmed the biblical view as to the nature of man and his need.

Man's basic nature has not changed in the last two thousand years.
Man with all his technological and scientific progress is essentially the
same as he was in the first century. This time in our lives is not called
the "Age of Anxiety" or the "Era of the Aspirin" for nothing. "Something" is still wrong—seriously wrong—with modern man. The question is, can this "something" be dealt with or eradicated by man's
own efforts—education, technology, psychology, or social progress?
Evidence points otherwise. The most educated are still plagued with
this problem. The greatest scientists, through science alone, have not

eradicated the problem. The present situation affirms the biblical perspective, man is a sinner.

Man in his basic human nature does not naturally "love his neighbor as himself." He certainly does not naturally "love his enemies." The reality of sin in human experience is of such radical nature that man, in his own strength, is inadequate to deal with it. The remedy must come from God.

2. God's Action

According to Alexander Miller, "sin is terrible and redemption is costly." Alienation from God is so deep and so severe that the solution to man's problem cannot be found either in reason or in progress. Miller points out the fact that scientific progress has dispelled many of the ghosts that plagued religious man at an earlier age of history. This seems encouraging until we pause and consider that "men now fear the scientists more than they feared the ghosts." However, one who has an understanding of the biblical faith should not expect reason to be the ultimate solution to man's problems, ". . . for in biblical faith nature, reason and history are all perverted by a most radical distortion." Man is gripped in a tetanus-like death. "The self turns in upon the self" and thus contributes to his own self-destruction. He can be freed from this deathly cycle "only by the injection of some serum" which comes from outside of himself. Redemption cannot come through reason because the egocentricity with which man is afflicted "perverts all reason." Man cannot find deliverance through an act of his own will because his will "is intrinsically self-will" and this is the essence of man's problem, not the source of his solution. "There is no stance in the human psyche from which an attack can be leveled against this radical distemper, since the distemper poisons the whole self." This is why the Bible "calls not for a resolve but for a rescue." This is why, when the Bible speaks of man's fundamental problem, it speaks "not of progress but of the coming of a Messiah."[18]

God, in infinite love, has acted in behalf of man. Man's need is radical and God's solution is radical. He gave his Son. The pivotal verse here is the one which because of its familiarity too often fails to have anything like the significance for us it should have. "For God so loved the world, that he gave his only begotten Son, that whosoever believeth in him should not perish, but have everlasting life" (John 3:16). Paul says, "God was in Christ, reconciling the world unto himself" (2 Cor. 5:19). He who knew no sin bore our sins "in his own body" (1 Pet. 2:24). Concerning his own mission Jesus said, "The Son of man came not to be ministered unto, but to minister, and to give his life a ransom for many" (Mark 10:45). God, in Christ, has acted mightily in behalf of man. In this act God revealed to man the sinfulness of his sin and provided a way of salvation. In this act God was expressing his infinite love and was wooing man back to himself.

Man must become a "new man." This re-creation, however, cannot come from within; it must come from outside man—from him who created man in the first place. As Jesus said in his conversation with Nicodemus, man must "be born again" (or "be born from above") (John 3:3). Or as Paul says, he must become a "new creation" (2 Cor. 5:17). It is this work of God that gives man a new meaning for life, a new center for life, a new motivation for life, and a new direction for life.

3. The Personal

However God does not force this re-creation upon us, nor does he give it without our being aware of it. Man must respond to God's invitation. Salvation is freely offered, but we must accept that which is offered. It is true that God comes in many ways, but ultimately our relationship with God involves conscious, voluntary choice. Salvation involves both the work of God in Christ and the personal response.

Regardless of what view a person takes concerning sacraments, the personal element in the salvation relationship cannot be ignored or minimized. Repentance and forgiveness which heal the brokenness in man come in a personal relationship of the profoundest possible kind. Reconciliation with God through Christ is always individual and personal. To emphasize the individual and personal aspects of this relationship is not to deny that there are also corporate and social aspects to the salvation relationship. What I am saying here is that for this experience to be dynamic and meaningful each individual must make his own response. It cannot be done by proxy—not ultimately. At some time the individual must choose for himself. Likewise it must be a personal choice; that is, it must be an intelligent and conscious choice. If the experience is really going to be internal rather than external and if the experience is really going to be deeply meaningful rather than superficial, then each person, in his own context, must meet the living Lord and make his own choice, his own response.

Man's decision determines his destiny. "He that believeth on him is not condemned: but he that believeth not is condemned already, because he hath not believed in the name of the only begotten Son of God" (John 3:18). This preserves man's freedom, but the necessity of personal choice does not deny the fact of God's divine initiative in coming to man. Neither does God's initiative deny the necessity of a personal response. The salvation relationship not only involves man's initial response to God, it also involves man's continuing response to God. This is not a "one time and you've had it" affair. The continuing response is as essential as the initial response. Or it might be said that the continuing response is an evidence of the sincerity and genuineness of the initial response.

The importance of the personal is also demonstrated in church history. When religion becomes impersonal and external it loses its dynamic and becomes a dull, prosaic routine. It was against this type of lifeless religion that both Martin Luther and John Wesley rebelled. And today, it is against this type of lifeless religion we must rebel. On the other hand, every time there was a great upsurge of religion in the history of the church, one of the central characteristics of such a period was that religion became personal, experiential, and relational.

Even Walter Rauschenbusch, the chief apostle of the social gospel movement, emphasized the necessity of individual, personal salvation. He recognized that each person is a sinner and "the salvation of the individual is . . . an essential part of salvation." He said, "Every new being is a new problem of salvation." Granted that the evangelistic emphasis of the past had certain limitations, "our discussion cannot pass personal salvation by."[19] It is exceedingly unfortunate that forces and factors developed which caused this emphasis of Rauschenbusch to be lost, so that the social gospel movement came to emphasize a social salvation only. Had it not done so the recent history of the church in the United States might have been drastically different.

In experiential religion, nothing can take the place of the personal. This in no way is intended to minimize the work of God in the totality of these experiences. It is simply a recognition of the imperative necessity of man's personal and continuing response to the living Lord. Many nominal Christians have discovered the futility and inadequacy of a secondhand type of faith and a dull, routine expression of religion. This is the testimony of so many who are crying out for renewal today. Their testimony is, "I grew up in the church. I joined the church (or was confirmed) when I was a child. I went to college and left the church for a while. Then I got married and eventually came back to the church. In church I taught Sunday school; I worked with the youth, and I served on the various committees or boards. But I really did not know what Christianity was all about. My religion had little or no meaning for me."

The only way for this to change is for religion to become deeply and intensely personal. Man must not only "come alive" in God; God must "come alive" in man. It is this "aliveness" that is so desperately needed in contemporary religion. Neither sacraments (in their tradition) nor routine institutional observances (in the Free Church tradition) automatically provide this dimension in religion. This is a personal dimension, and it is an absolute essential in dynamic religion.

4. *What Salvation Involves*

At least a part of what is involved in salvation is that a person comes to see more clearly than ever before who he is and who God is, and in this insight he makes the profound decision in which he surrenders his life to the sovereignty of God. In effect he changes "gods" in his life. Previously self was "god." Thus he could say, "I'll do as *I* please. I'll live life as *I* please." Now, in face to face encounter with God, he comes to say, "My Lord and my God." In this experience he finds forgiveness, reconciliation, redemption—God's free gift.

In this exchange of "gods" in which God is accepted as sovereign, we can no longer say, "I'll do as *I* please." We recognize that we are no longer "our own," because we have been "bought with a price." Now we say, "Thy will be done." Yet this surrender of life is not a surrender to a negative bondage. It is a joyful, free, exuberant surrender to the fullness and the fulfilling of life. It is the voluntary response to God's call to life!

What, then, is involved in this "call" to life—this "call" to be a part of "God's people"? It is a call to be a "holy priesthood" (Exod. 19:6, 1 Pet. 2:5, 9). Our calling is to fulfill the mission in which God is engaged in the world. The call to be a part of his people in effect is the call to join God's army and become dynamically and aggressively involved in his mission in the world. As is indicated in the Lord's Prayer which we so glibly recite, we are to give ourselves to

causing his will to be done on "earth as it is in heaven" (Matt. 6:10).
What is God's will that we are to do? He is seeking the redemption
of all men. "Not willing that any should perish, but that all should
come to repentance" (2 Pet. 3:9). This is a part of his will. But also
God wants the blind to see, the lame to walk, the sick to be healed. He
does not want any of his creatures to be hungry, or cold, or unclothed
(Matt. 25:35). He does not want any to suffer injustice, alienation,
and rejection (Mic. 6:8). This, too, is God's will that must be done.

The point is, God's call to salvation and to mission is one and the
same. According to the Bible, salvation and mission are two sides of
the same coin. A person can't have one without the other. "Not
every one that saith unto me, Lord, Lord, shall enter into the kingdom
of heaven; but he that doeth the will of my Father which is in
heaven" (Matt. 7:21).

Here is a "package deal" and a person takes all or nothing. This is
what "salvation" means in the New Testament. To have "faith" means
that a person not only "believes in" but "commits himself to" this
God—who is also Father. He commits himself to the way of God
even though obedience involves appalling risk and potential conflict.
This does not mean that the "new born" Christian "has arrived."
Certainly he does not achieve full maturity in this initial experience.
There will be many experiences of growth—some victories and some
failures. However, the basic pattern, the basic direction, the essence of
this "new life in Christ" is present in this initial experience. To follow
this way, to express this life, to engage in this mission and ministry
is not optional for the one who is "in Christ." It is to this he is
called. It is to this he must respond.

CAUTIONS FOR THE EVANGELICAL EMPHASIS

That there have been serious and tragic mistakes made in the name
of "evangelism" is without question. The sooner these weaknesses are
identified and the more honest one is in admitting and facing them,
the better will be the chances of overcoming them. Often what has
"turned people off" and what they have criticized has not actually
been an evangelical emphasis but a distorted and perverted view of it.

1. *Superficial View of Salvation*

One of the major weaknesses has to do with the doctrine of salvation and the nature of the salvation relationship. There is a tendency on the part of some to have a view of salvation that is too shallow and superficial. In their zeal to get people "saved" they want to make it as easy as possible. This is quite understandable and we can agree with this desire. There is certainly no desire to make salvation unnecessarily difficult. However, in seeking to make it "easy" great care must be exercised not to pervert the biblical meaning of salvation.

There are three major expressions of this tendency to view salvation too superficially, all of which are interrelated. There is the tendency to view man from the perspective of Greek philosophy rather than from the Hebrew or biblical perspective. Greek philosophy viewed man as a dualism—"soul" and "body." The Hebrew-biblical view is that man is a unity—a "living soul." Following Greek philosophy, these people are primarily interested in getting man's "soul" saved. This is accomplished by getting the individual to "accept Christ" and make a "profession of faith." Of course, in honesty, they would like to see the person's life changed also. But from their perspective the "big job" is to get the "soul" saved. Their major emphasis is on "souls." With great zeal they go around contacting people, seeking to get them to "accept" and to "profess." Once the person has "accepted" and "professed," they move on and try to get another "soul" saved. It's "souls for eternity" that occupies their attention. And they fail to understand that their whole view of salvation is based on an erroneous foundation of Greek philosophy rather than upon biblical concepts.

With this view it is easy to see why these people place almost exclusive emphasis on an individual's initial decision. It is also possible to understand why they have a minimum of emphasis upon life here and now. If their view of man is correct, that is, if Greek philosophy is correct so that it is possible for a man's "soul" to be saved while his "body" (life here and now) remains relatively unchanged, then a case could be made for their approach to evangelism. If, on the other hand, the Hebrew-biblical view of man is correct, that is, man is a unity—"a living soul"—then man, if he is saved at all, is saved as a totality. A part of him cannot be saved while another part of him is not. If the Hebrew-biblical concept of man is correct, then the approach of those who emphasize a narrow view of evangelism is erroneous.

It is true that there are passages in the New Testament that seem to imply that salvation is quite simple: "Whosoever shall not receive the kingdom of God as a little child, he shall not enter therein"

(Mark 10:15). On the other hand, there are passages that imply salvation is quite difficult: "Whosoever he be of you that forsaketh not all that he hath, he cannot be my disciple" (Luke 14:33). This simply means that we must take into account the whole of the New Testament in determining the nature of the salvation relationship. The fact is, salvation is both simple and difficult. We must not try to make it either one or the other.

This reveals another trap into which some committed to an evangelical emphasis sometime fall. They select a few passages which become for them "the plan of salvation." Because these passages are taken from the Bible, they feel theirs is a biblical view of salvation. But they fail to take into consideration other passages—which, incidentally, are just as biblical—that emphasize other aspects of the salvation experience. For example, they may say, "What did Paul reply to the Philippian jailer when he cried, 'What must I do to be saved'? He replied only, 'Believe on the Lord Jesus Christ, and thou shalt be saved.' That's all a person needs to know. All a person needs to do is 'believe.'" If we understood and meant all that Paul did when he used the term "believe," this would be one thing. But to take the statement at face value, with whatever meaning, or lack of it, a person might put into the word "believe," is much too simplistic an approach. The same word means different things to different people.

On the one hand, salvation may seem to be quite simple. The Bible says, "Except ye repent, ye shall all likewise perish" (Luke 13:3). "For God so loved the world, that he gave his only begotten Son, that whosoever believeth in him should not perish, but have everlasting life" (John 3:16). "But as many as received him, to them gave he power to become the sons of God, even to them that believe on his name" (John 1:12). "That if thou shalt confess with thy mouth the Lord Jesus, and shalt believe in thine heart that God hath raised him from the dead, thou shalt be saved. For with the heart man believeth unto righteousness; and with the mouth confession is made unto salvation" (Rom. 10:9–10).

On the other hand, the Bible also says, "Every branch in me that beareth not fruit he taketh away" (John 15:2). "Whosoever will come after me, let him deny himself, and take up his cross, and follow me. For whosoever will save his life shall lose it; but whosoever shall lose his life for my sake and the gospel's, the same shall save it" (Mark 8:34–35). "If any man come to me, and hate not his father, and

mother, and wife, and children, and brethren, and sisters, yea, and his
own life also, he cannot be my disciple" (Luke 14:26). "Not every
one that saith unto me, Lord, Lord, shall enter into the kingdom of
heaven; but he that doeth the will of my Father which is in heaven"
(Matt. 7:21). "Then shall the King say unto them on his right hand,
Come, ye blessed of my Father, inherit the kingdom prepared for you
from the foundation of the world. . . . Inasmuch as ye have done it
unto one of the least of these my brethren, ye have done it unto me"
(Matt. 25:34, 40).

The whole of the Bible needs to be taken into account in seeking
to understand the meaning of the salvation relationship, not just
a few selected passages.

2. *A Witness through Words Alone*

As indicated earlier, I reject the emphasis on "deed" without
"words." However, the danger of those interested in an evangelical
emphasis is just the opposite. This is the danger of an emphasis on
"words" without "deed." It cannot be denied that the primary means
of witness by evangelicals in the immediate past has been through the
use of words—spoken and printed. From pulpits, in revival meetings,
in special evangelistic meetings, over the radio and television, through
tracts and newspapers, in so many ways the witness has been given
through words. The weakness is that the witness has not been given
adequately through deeds. In biblical times the Word "became flesh."
In our time the Word has become "words." The need of our time
is for "the Living Word" again to become flesh—our flesh. The Word
must again become incarnate—incarnate in us.

Christians ought to express genuine love and concern for other
persons simply because of God dwelling in them and because they
have needs. This should not be done as a means to an end or as a
strategy. Though it is relatively low on the hierarchy of motivations,
let me point out that to express God's love through action is one of
the most effective approaches to evangelism open to us today. It is
through the incarnate demonstration of love that an individual may
become motivated even to think about his relationship with God or to
care about God.

For example, two ladies read about a tragic automobile accident
that takes the life of the father of a family. The family lives in the
less desirable part of the city, but the two ladies go to the home and

introduce themselves to the mother. They say something like, "We read of your tragedy and want to express our sympathy. Is there anything we can do? Can we do some grocery shopping? Are there people to be notified? Can we help with the children? We are at your disposal. Use us any way you desire."

Unobtrusively they try to help in any way they can. Sometimes they simply sit and listen. Then when the day is over and the ladies start to leave, it would only be natural for the wife to express her appreciation. And in doing so, it is quite likely that she would ask, "Why did you ladies do this? You don't know me. Before today, you never even heard of me."

When the question, "Why?" is asked, the ladies can tell her about the God who does know her, who loves and cares for her, and who is seeking to express his love and care for her through them. When people ask why, we have a prime opportunity for witness. Our weakness today is that as Christians we are not living and ministering to people in such a way as to cause them to ask why. This is not the reason for demonstrating incarnate love and care for persons, but it is one of the bonuses—an opportunity for witness.

Also the "deed" is often a means God uses to help people understand the "words." For example, we say, "God loves you." For many, many people in our world this means absolutely nothing. They have never experienced a shred of love. Unwanted as children they were put out on the streets to shift for themselves. They were scolded and whipped and left alone and grew up fighting and getting beaten. When they became older, society took the place of parents as the one who whipped and against whom they fought. They got and lost jobs, usually through their own fault. What did they care? They had no motivation. There was nothing ahead for them except fighting. Then someone says to them, "God loves you." Their response is, "That's a laugh. Who is this God and what is this 'love' jazz?" If these people, and many who may not be quite this extreme, are ever going to have any serious understanding of God's love and what it means, they must first experience love in human terms—in us and through us.

This was the experience of one young lady who became involved in the life of an alcoholic prostitute. After demonstrating genuine concern on a very practical level (food and clothing) for a number of weeks, the lady finally persuaded the girl to go to an institution where she could get psychiatric help. She visited her several times each week in the institution. Finally after a number of months the doctor said the girl was ready to be an "outpatient." Where was she to go? There was nowhere but back to the streets. So the lady took the girl into her own home. After a number of weeks and episodes (failures and victories), the girl became sick. It wasn't possible to get her into the hospital because of crowded conditions. So the lady stayed up all night nursing the girl. In the morning when the girl was better, she said, "Tell me now about your God. If you had tried to tell me before, I wouldn't have listened. But since you have not given up on me, maybe I can believe that God hasn't given up on me either." It was a deed—a demonstration—that gave her an understanding of the love of God and also gave her hope.

3. *Manipulation*

Another criticism that is leveled at those who follow this evangelical emphasis is that manipulation is sometimes used to cause people to make a decision. Unfortunately this criticism too often has been founded on fact. Manipulation is something that has absolutely no place in the Christian enterprise. For an evangelical to use manipulation is a tacit denial of the power of God, the work of Christ, and the presence of the Holy Spirit. Manipulation in effect says, "I'm not sure God is able to get this decision by himself, so I must arrange it to make sure it happens." Manipulation is either an evidence of the arrogant pride of man (in which he tries to play God) or it is an evidence of utter lack of faith in God, or both.

What is meant by manipulation? What is the difference between "influence" which is legitimate and "manipulation" which is not legitimate? According to *Webster's Dictionary,* manipulation is "the act of operating upon skillfully for the purpose of giving a false appearance to; the giving of a special turn, direction, or color to for one's own purposes." Taking into account the religious dimension, I would say that manipulation is dealing with a person in such a way that his freedom and personhood are violated.

Unfortunately some evangelists, pastors, and religious workers seemingly are so concerned to build up their own reputations as "effective" evangelists that their major efforts are directed toward getting large numbers of "decisions" they can report to the appropriate papers. They have become extremely skillful in the use of certain "gimmicks," certain methods of extending the "invitation," certain procedures for eliciting "responses." These approaches smack of the worst type of crude and crass commercialism. They violate the basic principles of personhood by treating persons as things.

Jesus, in his life and ministry, never resorted to any such approaches. His dealing with the rich young ruler may be taken as example. The rich young ruler had many things in his favor. He was concerned about his condition and came inquiring of Jesus concerning eternal life. He was both moral and religious. Although he said he had kept the commandments, when Jesus laid down the condition (which, incidentally, was neither simple nor easy), the young man went away "very sorrowful" (Luke 18:23). Surely Jesus must have been attracted to this fine young man with all his potential. Yet there was no pressure, no manipulation. He left the young man completely free.

Here, again, we come to this matter of freedom. Freedom of choice is the very essence of Christian encounter. In the aloneness of the encounter in which an individual meets the Eternal God, there is a point beyond which a third man cannot and must not go. Parents, teachers, pastors, evangelists may help lead up to this experience, but there is a time when the individual meets God alone for himself. No outside person must violate the sacredness of this personal encounter by invading it and seeking to manipulate the response. This is something not even God himself does. He leaves the individual free. To be truly a person, he must be free, even free to reject.

On the other hand, we must not go to the opposite extreme. In our desire to avoid manipulation we must not withdraw and do nothing to express our care and concern for the person who stands in need of redemption. This can become for us a cloak behind which we hide to excuse our failure to express in any active, positive way our concern for man in his relationship with God. In terms of the total church members in Protestant churches, the sin of the few is that they have been guilty of manipulation. But this is certainly not the greatest sin nor the greatest danger facing Protestantism today. The sin of the large majority of church members is they have not given any witness at all. Sometimes they have sought to salve their consciences for this failure by pointing the accusing finger at the sin of the few. Consequently, in our ministry to people we must find that balance between demonstrating a deep and genuine concern for a person and at the same time leaving him a free human being. We are to trust God to do his work.

There is another area in which every effort must be made to avoid manipulation. This has to do with our relationship with young children. A pastor, teacher, or evangelist simply must not pressure children into making decisions when they are not sufficiently mature to make them. This is a highly emotional and complex issue. It involves the nature of the salvation relationship. Granted that a person is "saved by grace, through faith" and not by knowledge, yet it is obvious that some knowledge is necessary in an authentic salvation experience. How much, then, does one need to know about God, about himself, about the life to which God is calling to make this an authentic relationship? This involves developmental psychology. How mature does a person have to be before he can begin to comprehend abstractions? (God is a Spirit.) And more importantly, how mature does a person have to be before he can make a responsible, lifelong decision that involves the totality of his existence?

The salvation relationship also involves personal experiences which are very meaningful to the persons who have had them. There are those who say they were "saved" at a very early age. Their report is that they knew what they were doing. On the other hand, my testimony is just the opposite. I joined the church and was baptized at a relatively early age and I didn't know what I was doing. I have talked with literally hundreds of young people who "made professions of faith" when they were young children, and the testimony of large numbers is that they, too, did not know what they were doing. It was only after they became more mature that they began to grapple responsibly with their relationship with God.

No attempt is made here to give a solution to this problem. The issue before us is manipulation. It is relatively easy to manipulate an immature child. We can secure the desired response by the way we talk to him, put our arm around him, phrase our questions. In special meetings we can gather children together and "talk" to them in such a way as to get the desired response. But in so doing we have violated their personhood. We have manipulated them. This we must not do.

4. *Exploitation*

Those who have followed a social emphasis also sometimes question the reality, the depth, and the genuineness of the evangelical's concern for people. They ask, are the evangelicals truly concerned for people as human beings? Thus they raise a crucial question as to motivation.

When the evangelicals do engage in social ministry to persons, do they do so because of a genuine care and concern for persons or is this social ministry simply another "gimmick" used to "hook" persons for an evangelistic purpose? Those committed to the social emphasis charge that when the evangelical motive is dominant (or even when it is present), the social service rendered to people in their need is in reality an insidious means of exploiting persons rather than serving them. They also charge that the evangelicals have simply made a large number of "rice" Christians out of the underprivileged. These people make "professions of faith" and attend the meetings in storefront buildings or missions simply for the food and clothing they get.

These charges are not without basis in fact. The evangelicals will have to admit that at times (certainly not all the time) some of their adherents, either because of their zeal or their theology, or both, have treated persons as evangelistic objects rather than as human beings. There was not a genuine concern for persons. People were objects to be used for the benefit of the church as an institution or in behalf of the evangelistic enterprise. For example, a pastor and deacon were engaged in conversation about the deacon's fellow worker at the factory. The deacon was telling of the overwhelming difficulties and problems being encountered by this fellow worker. Finally the pastor said, "Why don't you seek to be a minister to him in this time of need?" Without thinking the deacon replied, "Why? He lives clear across town. He'll never join our church."

Therefore we must face the question: for the one who is committed to the proposition that every man needs a personal relationship with Christ, is it really possible to serve another in the physical-social areas with a genuine motive of concern for the person as a person, or must the motive inevitably be distorted? Not only is it possible, but for the Christian it is an absolute necessity for both of these emphases to be held in proper balance.

Those who are called to be the People of God must have a genuine love and concern for persons as persons. Our love for persons and our ministry to them must never be conditioned by their response to us. This is the nature of God's love for man—it is unconditional. God comes to man, loving him, serving him, ministering to him regardless of his response. And God keeps on loving and ministering to man regardless of whether he ever responds or not. As the People of God we must care for man as God cares for him. Remembering that man is a physical-social being, we must care for him and minister to him as a physical-social being. This means that we will minister to man in his human needs regardless of response—regardless of whether he ever says "thank you" or not. And we must keep on ministering to these people in their human-social needs whether they ever make any response or not. "Love never quits." We must love man and minister to him simply because he is a human being.

At times we will minister to man in places and situations where an evangelistic response is not even possible. For example, here is a Christian on the board of education who gives himself with abandon to the task of improving education for the underprivileged, the slow learners, and the retarded. Or here is a Christian on the board of aldermen or the city council who works with vigor and at real personal sacrifice to eliminate the substandard housing in the city. These men may never even meet the beneficiaries of their efforts. They are concerned for persons as human beings, and as an expression of their Christian commitment they seek to minister to these people.

However, if we are committed to the task of leading people to be "fully human," we must be vitally concerned about man's relationship with God. It is only as a person comes to know the meaning of life as revealed in God through Jesus Christ that he can become "fully" human. If we are interested in ministering to the "whole man," as those committed to the social emphasis insist, then we must minister to him in terms of the spiritual dimension of his life. My quarrel with those committed to a social ministry alone is that they are guilty of ministering to only a part of man. As Thomas Merton said, "To reconcile man with man and not with God is to reconcile no one at all. It is the old problem of the Social Gospel over again."[20] A person cannot find his full humanity or discover wholeness unless he finds it in God.

To hold in balance this dual emphasis, a concern for man as a human being and a concern for him as a spiritual being, is to follow the example of Jesus. Instance after instance could be cited to demonstrate his concern for the physical needs of man. On the other hand, Jesus also said, "The Son of man is come to seek and to save that which was lost" (Luke 19:10). One incident in the ministry of Jesus that illustrates his dual concern is the healing of the man with the palsy. On the one hand, Jesus said to him, "Son, thy sins be forgiven thee" (Mark 2:5). But Jesus also healed his sickness, saying, "Arise, and take up thy bed, and go thy way into thine house" (Mark 2:11). Not to care for and minister to man in his human needs is to treat him as an object—something less than a human being. Yet since man is also a spiritual being, not to meet this need is not to meet him at the point of his deepest need.

NOTES

1. Robert Raines, *The Secular Congregation* (New York: Harper & Row, 1968), pp. 1–21.

2. Elton Trueblood, *The New Man for Our Time* (New York: Harper & Row, 1970), pp. 15–35.

3. Ibid., p. 25.

4. Elizabeth O'Connor, *Journey Inward, Journey Outward* (New York: Harper & Row, 1968), p. 9.

5. Ibid., p. 19.

6. William Stringfellow, *My People Is the Enemy* (New York: Holt, Rinehart & Winston, 1964), pp. 2–3.

7. Dr. F. G. Sampson, pastor, Mount Lebanon Baptist Church, Louisville, Kentucky.

8. William Muehl, "To Hell with Acceptance," *Reflection, A Journal of Opinion at Yale Divinity School* 64 (March, 1967):14.

9. Ibid.

10. H. H. Farmer, *Revelation and Religion* (London: Nisbet & Co., Ltd., 1954), p. 109.

11. H. H. Farmer, *The World and God* (London: Nisbet & Co., Ltd., 1935), p. 255.

12. A much more adequate treatment of this issue is found in John R. Claypool, *The Problem of Hell in Contemporary Theology.* Doctoral dissertation, Southern Baptist Theological Seminary, Louisville, Ky., 1959. See especially pp. 44–50, 63–72, 80–81, 93, 197–250.

13. Raines, *The Secular Congregation,* p. 11.

14. Claypool, pp. 201–16.

15. Nels F. S. Ferré, *The Christian Understanding of God* (New York: Harper & Row, 1951), p. 230.

16. The term *evangelical* is not used here in the more limited sense of the neo-Calvinist evangelicals. It assumes rather the historic Protestant meaning of those who emphasize personal concern and commitment.

17. George W. Forrell, *The Protestant Faith* (Englewood Cliffs, N. J.: Prentice-Hall, 1960), pp. 142–43.

18. Alexander Miller, *The Renewal of Man* (Garden City, N. Y.: Doubleday & Co., 1955), pp. 56–59.

19. Walter Rauschenbusch, *A Theology for the Social Gospel* (New York: Macmillan, 1918), pp. 95–96.

20. Thomas Merton, "Events and Pseudo-Events," *Katallagete* (Summer 1966), p. 11.

CHAPTER FOUR

The Nature of
God's Mission (continued)

U p to this point we have had a lively discussion on the necessity for an emphasis on evangelism. Now I want to write with equal vigor concerning the necessity for an emphasis on social concern and action. Unfortunately, those who traditionally have been committed to an emphasis on evangelism are victims of a paralyzing fear complex when it comes to any social emphasis in the church. There has been violent opposition and rejection on the part of many. Others say, "It is not so much that I am against social concern, but every time the church starts magnifying a social emphasis, there is a serious decline in the emphasis on evangelism. Look at what happened during the social gospel movement." Or as one pastor said to me, "I have never seen a church that was deeply committed to social action that was also seriously involved in personal evangelism." This statement could easily be challenged, but let it illustrate a viewpoint. Their position is that an emphasis on social involvement tends to lead to a perversion of the gospel.

My reply is that if they are going to eliminate from emphasis anything that has contributed to a perversion of the gospel, they will have to eliminate almost everything in the gospel. One of the first things they would have to eliminate is evangelism itself. Throughout the history of the church certain emphases on evangelism have been one of the major causes of perversion in the life of the church. Certain views of the humanity of Jesus have perverted the gospel, as have particular views concerning his deity. Occasionally, views of the Holy Spirit have perverted the gospel, as have certain views of God. Certain views as to the nature of the church as well as to the nature of the Christian life have led to perversion in the church. Yet no one would even dare to suggest that we should eliminate an emphasis on God, Jesus, the Holy Spirit, the nature of the church, and the nature of the Christian life because they might lead to a perversion of the gospel. Thus, to reject an emphasis on social concern and action because it *might* lead to a perversion of the gospel is based on inadequate and illogical thinking. *Indeed, to omit an emphasis on social involvement is a perversion of the gospel!*

This takes us to the even more serious problem of the evangelical who rejects the social emphasis. In doing so, it seems to me, he is actually saying that he does not believe the *whole* gospel. He believes only a part of it—the *evangelical* part. Apparently, he believes that it would be good if both the evangelical and the social emphases could be held in proper balance, but he doesn't *really* think this is possible. Consequently, he says, "Let's emphasize that which is more important, the 'spiritual' (or evangelistic) aspect." But what this attitude really indicates is that he does not believe the whole gospel is possible, so he chooses the part he wants to emphasize. *This is a brazen lack of faith in the gospel on the part of the evangelical!* I deny the assumption that an emphasis on the whole gospel is an impossibility. Not only is it possible and practical; an emphasis on anything else is a perversion of the gospel.

INADEQUACY OF EVANGELICAL EMPHASIS ALONE

1. *Salvation Tends to Be Too Individualistic*

Let me state it clearly. Salvation is personal and individual. This emphasis on the personal dimension of the Christian experience has been a primary strength in the evangelical emphasis. The lack of an emphasis on the personal has been a vital weakness on the part of the so-called "liberals." However, for the evangelical this emphasis on the personal and individual has tended to become warped so that salvation becomes increasingly individualistic. That is, while the vertical, God-man relationship is essential in the salvation relationship, the evangelical comes to view this as the *totality* of the salvation relationship. "My God and I" is the theme of this view. The weakness is not that this emphasis on the personal is erroneous; the weakness is that the personal relationship with God is understood to be the *whole* of the Christian experience.

This tendency toward an individualistic view of salvation is seen in many gospel songs. A scanning of the table of contents of many song books will reveal that a large majority of songs deal only with the individual's relationship with God.[1] One that was a favorite when I was young is entitled, "In the Garden." The chorus went like this:

> And He walks with me, and He talks with me,
> And He tells me I am His own;
> And the joy we share as we tarry there,
> None other has ever known.

Here is clearly illustrated the emphasis on the close, personal relationship between an individual and God. This emphasis on a personal relationship was—and still is—very meaningful to me. But I must confess that during my youth while this personal relationship was being emphasized no corresponding emphasis was given about my concern for and relationship to society. The only emphasis on other people was to be concerned about their "souls"—to get them saved. We seldom sang, "Where Cross the Crowded Ways of Life," or "I Walked Today Where Jesus Walked." In most hymn books there is a dearth of hymns that deal with social issues. Only now are some being written.

In emphasizing the individual aspects of sin and salvation the evangelical has failed to understand and stress adequately the corporate aspects of sin and salvation. This is another of those areas where there was fear that if one aspect was emphasized the other would be neglected. Thus the evangelical with his deep (and correct) concern for the personal emphasis feared that, if any serious emphasis was placed on the factor of the solidarity of the race and on the corporate aspects of sin and salvation, the personal element would either be neglected or omitted. There is evidence that this fear has a basis in fact.

However, the gospel demands that both emphases be held in proper balance. Sin is personal; thus each individual is guilty of sin. But sin is also social. The individual is a sinner because he participates in an economic order that pollutes the water and air for profit. Thus in addition to our individual sin and guilt we all also share in a solidarity of sin and guilt.

Salvation is personal and must be personal. Each individual must come into a personal relationship with God. However, salvation is also social. God not only wants to save individuals; he also wants to save the world. That is, he wants to save the totality of the created order.

He desires to be Lord of all. This means he desires to be Lord of politics, economics, education—all areas of life. This is a large part of what Jesus had in mind in a portion of the Lord's prayer, "Thy will be done on earth as it is done in heaven." It is true that to redeem social structures does not mean that individuals will automatically be saved. On the other hand, it should be noted that to save individuals does not automatically change the social order. Halford Luccock pointed out that if everyone in town dug a well in his backyard, the result would not be a municipal water system.

I read about a Christian who was walking down the street in the slum area of one of our major cities. He saw a man, apparently struck by a car, lying in the gutter. If this had been in biblical times the Good Samaritan would have bound up his wounds and taken him to the hospital. But today it is against the law to move an injured person on the city streets. So the Christian did what the law allowed; he telephoned for an ambulance and waited with the injured man. The ambulance service, being what it is in that particular city, especially in the slum area, took an hour to get there. The man died on the way to the hospital. In such a situation what is the Christian to do? Is he simply to stand by injured people waiting for the ambulance to come? No! If a person wants to be a Christian in this kind of civilization, he must work to improve the ambulance service! Individual salvation will not solve this problem. This is a social problem, and it demands the redemption of this part of the structures of society. The Christian must come to understand that although salvation is individual and personal, he cannot be fully whole so long as there is brokenness anywhere in God's world!

2. *The Christian Life Tends to Be Too Moralistic*

When the emphasis is on individual salvation, the Christian life tends to be expressed primarily in terms of personal piety and individual morality—kindness, thoughtfulness, honesty, devotion to family, faithfulness in family relationships, etc. These people are recognized as being among the finest people in the community. Again, it must be pointed out that this emphasis on personal morality is highly desirable; indeed, it is essential, but too often this is accompanied by an inadequate social consciousness and concern. Their religion has magnified personal morality but not social concern. Consequently, it is possible for one who is highly moral personally, who is faithful to his wife, and who is honest in his business to drive through a ghetto each morning on his way to work and never have a twinge of conscience nor relate it to his Christian commitment. Or a highly respected leader in the church could own slum housing and never see any relationship between this and his "religion." They can live in the midst of wrong and not feel guilty because of it nor even be sensitive to it. For them there is a strange separation of personal morality and social responsibility. For them, "to be religious" is related to their personal lives and means personal morality. Social problems come in another category. These issues are "practical problems" and have little or nothing to do with religion.

3. *Christian Service Tends to Be Too Institutionally Oriented*

For the evangelical whose religion is almost exclusively directed toward God and who has such a limited concern for society, it is natural that his "service" for God should be primarily, if not wholly, oriented around the church.[2] As a rule, evangelicals are exceedingly active in the service they seek to render. They demonstrate deep dedication, and often real sacrifice in time and energy is expended in expressions of Christian service. The weakness is that their ministry is related almost exclusively to the church as an institution, and the world is sadly neglected.

For example, great emphasis is placed on tithing by these people. Often they give quite sacrificially. However, the money given is frequently used almost exclusively for "church" purposes. Little of it goes to meet human need. Rather, large amounts are sunk into larger and more plush church buildings. At times it seems that Christians today are trying to convince God that they love him by building bigger buildings rather than by serving people in the world. By erecting buildings, laymen and pastors sometimes deceive themselves into believing that they are serving God and being "religious." This is something they can do simply by giving money, and it demands a minimum of personal involvement. The cathedrals of Europe, beautiful though they are, stand as a constant reminder of the futility of such an effort. Yet we are in danger of duplicating this error.

Institutionally oriented Christians are often involved in vigorous visitation programs. They do go outside the church, however, the purpose of this "going" is to get people to come to the church. Now, I certainly am not opposed to people coming to church, so I feel this emphasis on visitation is highly commendable. But the weakness is that, church oriented as they are, they have no ministry for those who don't come to church. And I firmly believe that people should be cared for and ministered to whether or not they ever come to church.

However, with this church-oriented emphasis it is not surprising that many have come to believe the primary place in which a person serves God is *within* the church. Pastors and members of the church staff who are responsible for the organized life of the church have contributed to this notion. An announcement in a recent church bulletin read, "A course will be offered for those who are not now serving in the church in a church-elected position." The implication, of course, was that if you really want to serve God you ought to get prepared to serve in a church position. Service outside the church does not really "count." In fact one's service outside the church may come into conflict with service in the church. Frequently, dedication is measured by a person's willingness to give up some of his outside ministries in order to work in the church.

In this way the church tends to become identified with the kingdom of God. The feeling is that the kingdom is extended as the church (institution) is built. So all effort is given to building the church as an institution, and the world is either neglected or forgotten. These are some of the weaknesses that have developed when the emphasis has been only on personal salvation.

THE NECESSITY FOR A SOCIAL EMPHASIS

The emphasis on the physical-social needs of man is not simply a "desirable addition" to a gospel which at its base is "spiritual." The point here is that this social emphasis is just as integral and necessary a part of the gospel as the evangelical emphasis. Those who insist that the basic task of the church is to "save souls" are just as wrong in their view as are those who believe that the primary task is to meet the human needs of man. Either emphasis alone—or out of proportion—is inadequate.

One of the most hopeful signs on the horizon today is the fact that this dual emphasis increasingly is being made by those who formerly have been polarized at the extremes. For example, Sherwood Wirt, editor of *Decision,* a publication of the Billy Graham Evangelistic Association, has written an excellent book entitled *The Social Conscience of the Evangelical,* in which he extended a vigorous call to evangelicals to recognize the necessity for an emphasis on the social aspects of life. He said pointedly, "Any evangelism which ignores social concern is by its nature an incomplete and unscriptural evangelism."[3]

On the other hand Stephen C. Rose, who has been considered one of the "radical" liberals, has written, "Essentially, believing that man is the measure of all things, liberals have been tried and found wanting. . . . They are cast loose with no anchor of faith and no authority for guidance." The fundamentalists likewise have tended to be sterile —"believing" but without any adequate social response. What we need now, he said, is "a new synthesis based on a wedding of the personal and the public, of justice with love, of God's law with man's. What is needed is a social evangelicalism."[4]

In the same vein, Professor John Bright, long recognized and respected for his scholarship, said, "Exactly here is the relationship of social gospel to the gospel of individual salvation, and it is important that we get it. The two are not to be set apart as has so often been done, for they are two aspects of the same thing. Indeed, they are as intimate to each other as the opposite sides of the same coin. We can no longer, as 'liberals' have done, preach the ethics of Jesus and leave aside his person and work as if it were a cumbrous and superfluous theological baggage. At least if we do so, we must know that we do not preach the Jesus of the New Testament faith. Nor can we, as 'conservatives' have tended to do, sneer at the 'liberal' for not preaching a full gospel and then, because we urge men to salvation through faith, feel no need even to confront ourselves and our people with the demands of the righteousness of the Kingdom. This, too, is not to preach the Christ of the New Testament, but an incomplete Christ. We have not two gospels, social and personal, which vie for the limelight. We have one gospel, the gospel of the Kingdom of God, and it is both. We have simply nothing else to preach."[5]

To hold both of these emphases in proper tension and balance is no easy task. Individuals, by virtue of their backgrounds, interests, and personalities tend to be more concerned about one or the other. One of the primary weaknesses of the church throughout its history has been precisely at this point. At times it has emphasized one, and at times it has emphasized the other. Periods when these emphases were held in proper balance have been exceedingly rare. But to say that they *cannot* be in proper balance is a denial of the gospel! It is this that the gospel demands! This is our challenge today—to make this balance a reality!

1. *Biblical Basis*

In an examination of the necessity of a social emphasis in the life and ministry of the church, there are two questions that need to be asked. First, from a biblical perspective, is it imperative that social action have an equal emphasis along with personal evangelism? Second, is there any conflict between an emphasis on personal salvation and on social involvement? It is to the first question we now turn our attention.

There is no difficulty in finding biblical evidence for a profound social concern and involvement. In the early laws that governed Israel, careful instructions were given relative to the care that should be given to strangers, orphans, widows, the poor, and to hired servants (Deut. 14:28–29, 15:1–11, 24:14–22). "The early Hebrews learned at the foot of Mount Sinai that in the sight of God there is indeed a difference between the sacred and the profane, but there is no difference between the spiritual and the social."[6]

The social concern of the prophets is well known. After a vehement condemnation of the people for their sin and failure, God calls for repentance, and this repentance is in social terms. "Your hands are full of blood. Wash ye, make you clean; put away the evil of your doings from before mine eyes; cease to do evil; Learn to do well; seek judgment, relieve the oppressed, judge the fatherless, plead for the widow" (Isa. 1:15b–17). Note that God did not call the people to be more "religious." Indeed it was the emptiness of their "religiousness" he condemned (Isa. 1:1–15). The fiery words of Amos sound as contemporary as the daily newspaper. He condemned war (1:11, 13), injustice (3:9–10), economic greed (2:6), gross immorality (2:7), the oppression of the poor (4:1, 5:11), bribery (5:12), and business deceit (8:5–6). The religious observances which the people were meticulous to observe were repudiated by God. He called upon them instead to observe justice and righteousness (Amos 5:24, also Isa. 1:1–17). Micah in his statement of the essence of religion placed emphasis on God's concern for man in his social relationships. "He hath shewed thee, O man, what is good; and what doth the Lord require of thee, but to do justly, and to love mercy, and to walk humbly with thy God?" (Mic. 6:8)

It would be possible to respond at this point by admitting that God is concerned about man in his personal and social relationships but it still does not prove whether social concern should have *equal* emphasis with personal evangelism. What does the New Testament have to say about this? More specifically, what does Jesus say about this? As has been indicated, it is true there are certain passages that emphasize personal salvation and "belief." To the inquiry by the Philippian jailer, "What must I do to be saved?" Paul responded, "Believe on the Lord Jesus Christ, and thou shalt be saved" (Acts 16:30–31). It must be recognized that this may not be all that Paul said to the jailer at this time. It is simply all that was recorded. It is not possible to put the *fullness* of the meaning of the gospel into one statement. If one seeks to sum up the entire gospel in one statement, then the meaning of this statement must be interpreted in light of the teachings concerning the total gospel. This is true even for the summary statement given by our Lord, "Thou shalt love the Lord thy God with all thy heart, and with all thy soul, and with all thy mind. This is the first and great commandment. And the second is like unto it, Thou shalt love thy neighbor as thyself" (Matt. 22:37–39). Note even here the dual emphasis on the personal and the social.

Thus in considering what is fundamental in the gospel relative to salvation, in addition to "believe" we must also give the most careful consideration to other passages where social involvement is emphasized as being central in the salvation relationship. In the parable of the two sons recorded in Matthew 21:28–32, the one son was condemned not because he did not "believe" but because he did not "go, work in my vineyard." When Jesus spoke the words of judgment, "The kingdom of God shall be taken from you," the reason given was not that they did not "believe." Their sin was that they had failed to "bring forth fruit" (Matt. 21:33–41). Also Jesus said that the kingdom would be given, not to those who "believed" better, but rather to those who would bring "forth the fruits thereof" (Matt. 21:43).

When a certain ruler came inquiring of Jesus, "What must I do to inherit eternal life?"—the same question the jailer asked of Paul—the reply of Jesus was not to "believe" but rather to "Sell all that thou hast, and distribute unto the poor . . . and come, follow me" (Luke 18:22). It is likely we have never heard an evangelistic sermon from this text. Thousands have been preached from Paul's reply, yet we neglect Jesus' reply. Again, Jesus, evidently in an attempt to explain what "believing" in him really meant, said, "Ye shall know them by their fruits" (Matt. 7:16). Also he said, "Not every one that saith unto me, Lord, Lord, shall enter into the kingdom of heaven; but he that doeth the will of my Father which is in heaven" (Matt. 7:21). Though we have only scratched the surface here, let one last reference suffice. In the parable of the Last Judgment the issue is quite clear. Those who entered the kingdom were those who had fed the hungry, given drink to the thirsty, clothed the naked, visited the sick and those in prison. Those who were rejected were those who failed to do these things. But when they protested that they did not know when they had failed to minister to him in these ways, his reply was, "Inasmuch as ye did it not to one of the least of these, ye did it not to me" (Matt. 25:31–46). This is not a salvation by works. Salvation is still God's gracious and free gift to man. But this does help explain what salvation means and what salvation involves.

The ministry of Jesus is a living demonstration of his concern for persons in their human need. In his first sermon preached at the beginning of his public ministry he selected a text from Isaiah, "The Spirit of the Lord is upon me, because he hath anointed me to preach the gospel to the poor; he hath sent me to heal the broken-hearted, to preach deliverance to the captives, and recovering of sight to the blind, to set at liberty them that are bruised, To preach the acceptable year of the Lord" (Luke 4:18–19). It is this, he said, he came to do.

When the disciples of John the Baptist came to Jesus inquiring whether he was the Promised One or should they look for another, the reply was basically in social terms. "Go your way, and tell John what things ye have seen and heard; how that the blind see, the lame walk, the lepers are cleansed, the deaf hear, the dead are raised, to the poor the gospel is preached" (Luke 7:22). One of his most burning teachings, given at the home of one of the chief Pharisees, had to do with how a "religious" person should relate to the poor and the outcast. "When thou makest a dinner or a supper, call not thy friends, nor thy brethren, neither thy kinsmen, nor thy rich neighbors; lest they also bid thee again, and a recompense be made thee. But when thou makest a feast, call the poor, the maimed, the lame, the blind: And thou shalt be blessed" (Luke 14:12–14a). It is well known, of course, that many of Jesus' miracles had to do with healing the sick, the blind, and the lame. Peter, looking back over the ministry of Jesus, described him as one who "went about doing good" (Acts 10:38).

This emphasis must be taken with the utmost seriousness. It is essential for the "in Christ" type of life. God's call is to mission. This mission is redemption. It is both personal and social—two sides of the same coin. We cannot have one without the other. When obedience in this area is lacking, God speaks in judgment, "Ye are not my people, and I will not be your God" (Hos. 1:9). Or if the words from

Jesus are preferred, "Why call ye me, Lord, Lord, and do not the things which I say?" (Luke 6:46). Again, "Many will say to me in that day, Lord, Lord, have we not prophesied in thy name? and in thy name have cast out devils? and in thy name done many wonderful works? And then will I profess unto them, I never knew you: depart from me, ye that work iniquity" (Matt. 7:22–23). These are sharp words, indeed. The answer to our first question is a resounding, *Yes!* According to the Bible the social emphasis must have equal emphasis along with personal evangelism.

2. *The Social Emphasis of the Evangelists from 1835 to 1865*

We now consider the second question: Is it possible to have a proper balance between an emphasis on personal salvation and on social involvement? One of the great fears of the evangelical is that a serious emphasis on social ills or social concerns will lead to a lack of emphasis on personal evangelism or personal salvation. The comment of a pastor quoted earlier is typical, "I have never seen a church that was deeply involved in social concerns that was also zealous in personal evangelism." It is this one fear, I believe, that is at the root of the lack of emphasis on social problems. Though I realize there are exceptions, in the main I think that most serious evangelicals are also concerned about people being exploited, about those who are cold and hungry living in indecent shacks. But they feel the "spiritual" condition of man is so much more important than the "physical" condition; they want to make sure that man's "major" need is met, namely, that he "be saved." This concept stems from a Greek view rather than from a Hebraic view of man. However, taking the evangelical's fear at face value, having a balanced emphasis on both personal evangelism and social involvement is not only a biblical necessity but a practical possibility.

I want to use the evangelists and the revival period between 1835 and 1865 as illustrative of this contention. Timothy L. Smith in an excellent book, *Revivalism and Social Reform,* called attention to a fact that has been lost or forgotten, namely, during the revivals of the mid-1800s it was the evangelists who were also among the leaders in social reform.[7] The loss of this knowledge has been tragic both for evangelical religion and for society. According to Smith, "Liberalism on social issues, not reaction, was the dominant note which evangelical preachers sounded before 1860. The most influential of them, from

Albert Barnes and Samuel Schmucker to Edward Norris Kirk and Matthew Simpson, defined carefully the relationship between personal salvation and community improvement."[8] As early as 1835, Edward Beecher wrote that the task of Christians was "not merely to preach the Gospel to every creature, but to reorganize human society in accordance with the law of God. To abolish all corruptions in religion and all abuses in the social system and, so far as it has been erected on false principles, to take it down and erect it anew."[9] Speaking of Wesley and the preachers associated with him in their great movement, Bready said, "To a phenomenal degree, these despised itinerant preachers were the heralds of a true Christian democracy; for, more than history has yet realized, did they release influences which have affected profoundly the sanest movements for social emancipation throughout the English-speaking world."[10]

There were, of course, reform movements and influences of a non-religious type during this period. But, according to Charles Cole, the religious reformers were primarily responsible for bringing about social changes. In the fight against poverty, delinquency, and other evils, and in the fight for temperance, women's rights, and antislavery, "those standing on the rock of piety" brought about these changes.[11] The Salvation Army emerged out of the revival of 1858–59, and throughout the years this group has demonstrated both a fervent evangelistic witness and a concern for persons in their social needs.

Nor was the social concern of the evangelists expressed for individuals only. Politics and social structures came in for their share of emphasis. It is true that fundamental in their ministry was the emphasis on the transformation of individual lives through personal conversion. However, these evangelists were not content simply to change individual lives. They attacked the evils of the day through the formation of societies and the mounting of national campaigns. The prison reform movement grew out of such concern. The number of the societies that were formed during this period "serves only to underline the close alliance between the planners of a new social and moral order and the more advanced followers of evangelical religion."[12]

Although it is not a widely recognized fact in our time, the evangelists of the mid-1800s were "far from disdaining earthly affairs." They "played a key role in the widespread attack upon slavery, poverty, and greed." And strange though it may seem, it was the evangelists, not the theological liberal, who "helped prepare the way both in theory and in practice for what later became known as the social gospel."[13]

Since slavery was the burning issue of the time, this was naturally a matter of major concern for the evangelists. Joshua Leavitt, head of *The Evangelist* in the 1830s, greatly popularized the abolitionist cause through his writings. George B. Cheever, a revered evangelist with deep concern for and commitment to personal evangelism, became deeply involved in numerous social concerns including slavery. Charles G. Finney did not become a crusader for the antislavery cause, but his sermons were filled with references to the problem. The depth of his commitment is demonstrated by the fact that "he would not become professor of theology at Oberlin until the trustees agreed to admit colored students."[14] It is said that he hid fugitive slaves in his attic.

John Wesley wrote and spoke with vigor condemning slavery in every form. He condemned the stealing of slaves from their native lands as worse than pagan heathenism, and he placed those who bought the slaves on the level with those who stole them. In reply to the argument that slavery was a legal, legitimate business Wesley asserted that human law could not turn "darkness into light or evil into good." Countering the argument that slavery was good for business, he said it would be better that England "remain uncultivated forever" than that her progress be built on such a despicable evil as slavery.[15] So deep were his feelings that the last letter Wesley wrote, just six days before his death, was addressed to William Wilberforce to encourage his continued violent opposition to slavery both in England and America.[16] "In summary, the revivalists seem to have carried the brunt of the religious attack upon the Negro's bondage. Especially after 1850, editors of denominational newspapers like Daniel Wise of Boston's *Zion's Herald* and George B. Cheever of *The Independent* helped bring about an awakening of conscience in the cities—then the focal points in the battle for men's minds. Albert Barnes, Gilbert Haven, Charles G. Finney, and scores of lesser men ably seconded them."[17]

The evangelists were also deeply concerned about the plight of the poor. The depth of Wesley's personal concern is demonstrated in one of his letters. "I have two silver spoons at London and two at Bristol. This is all the plate I have at present, and I shall not buy more while so many round me want bread."[18] According to his *Journal,* he gave to aid the destitute by providing food and clothing as he was able. But as a more positive and constructive approach he encouraged his followers not only to share their clothing with the poor but also to employ the women who were out of work to do sewing. They should be paid the "going wage" for their work and then given further assistance according to their need.[19] Again in his *Journal* Wesley wrote, "I visited as many more as I could. I found some in their cells underground; others in their garrets, half starved both with cold and hunger, added to weakness and pain. But I found not one of them unemployed who was able to crawl about the room. So wickedly, devilishly false is that common objection, 'They are poor only because they are idle.' "[20] His and other voices were also raised in condemnation of an industrial system that exploited the workers. In addition to seeking to minister to the poor individually, there were numerous institutional developments that sought to attack the problem of poverty from a broader base. Their wisdom is also seen in the fact that there were beginning efforts to identify and eliminate the causes of poverty.

There is further evidence that in addition to meeting the human needs of individuals the evangelists were deeply involved in seeking to change the laws and structures of society that permitted human exploitation. Those today who say that the only task of the minister is to "preach the gospel" would not have found support among the evangelists of the mid-nineteenth century. Henry Ward Beecher said, "It is the duty of the minister of the Gospel to preach on every side of political life. I do not say that he may; I say that he must."[21] Wesley was particularly vocal against the evils in the legal profession that he felt exploited the ignorant and the poor rather than giving them justice. On at least one occasion he condemned the lawyer for his lies and excesses more than the smuggler who was on trial.[22] His scathing pen was turned on numerous evils of the day. In speaking and writing, Wesley either directly or indirectly touched on practically every recognized social problem of his time. In every way open to him he sought to influence legislation, change social structures, and eliminate abuses.

In Wesley's preface to his 1739 Hymn Book he wrote, "The Gospel of Christ knows no religion but social, no holiness, but social holiness."[23] Bready concludes that "Wesley . . . was a mighty social reformer; for by initiating a marvelous spiritual movement latent with moral imperatives, he opened the springs of human sympathy and understanding, which in turn inspired and nourished a glorious succession of social reforms."[24]

What these evangelists did was not perfect, nor am I setting them up as models. They made mistakes, many of them. I am simply pointing out that here were men deeply committed to a personal, evangelical faith who were also deeply committed to social concern and involvement. The answer to our second question is also a resounding "Yes." It has been demonstrated that it is possible to have a balanced emphasis on both evangelism and social involvement.

CAUTIONS FOR THE SOCIAL EMPHASIS

We have discussed the weaknesses that are present when only the social is magnified in Christian ministry. In this section I want to indicate some cautions for those who have grown up in the evangelical tradition but who, because of the depth of their emerging social conscience, are now reacting against the evangelical position.

1. Over-react to Failures of the Past

For those who grew up in a tradition where personal salvation and personal evangelism were emphasized, there is danger they may become so fed up with what they see as "failures" of the past that in practice, if not in theology, they may throw out the whole evangelistic emphasis. First, there may be a reaction against what seems to be a superficial evangelistic methodology. They rebel against the "hard-line, buttonholing, 'are-you-saved' " approach. This is interpreted in terms of treating people as "things" rather than as human beings. It is felt that at least some who are engaged in this type of evangelism seem more interested in adding "spiritual scalps" to their "evangelistic belt" than they are in the welfare of the person. They have seen adults, young people, and small children manipulated into making so-called "professions." "Use the hard sell!" "Get them to sign on the dotted line!" These approaches have contributed toward a disillusionment with the whole evangelical emphasis.

Recently I was on a plane trip with a friend who is the pastor of a church. He is evangelical in his theology but is deeply sensitive in his social concern. We were talking about the decline in evangelistic emphasis in many churches. Then with deep feeling he said, "I know what you mean. I have to confess that I have become weak in this emphasis in my own ministry. Frankly, I am so fed up with our superficial approach, I don't do anything at all!" Those who feel this way don't want to deal superficially with people. They want to treat them as persons, help to build up relationships, and make friends. When they speak they don't want to speak superficially; the danger is they may never speak! Unfortunately, in relating to people in caring concern for their human needs, they never get around to presenting Christ.

In the second place, these over-reacters to past failures may react against a superficial view of evangelism and the Christian life. Because of their growing social sensitivity they feel and express a deep emotional repudiation of an evangelism that is concerned only with "saving the soul" and with life after death. The more they become aware of this life and this world with all its needs and possibilities the more they rebel against what they consider an approach to evangelism which is wholly inadequate. Yet, in looking about them in the churches, it is this approach to evangelism which seems to be the norm. Thus, responding to a negative reaction, they may throw up their hands in utter despair or simply "chuck the whole thing." The danger is in their becoming so "turned off" and alienated by the weaknesses in the evangelical approach that they may repudiate evangelism altogether. This would be tragic.

2. Become Caught Up in Social Involvement and Forget Evangelism

There is a grave danger in being so caught up with a social sensitivity and concern that authentic evangelism is ignored entirely. This may happen for a variety of reasons. For example, one might engage in social ministries with such enthusiasm and find so much personal fulfillment in ministering to the human needs of people he simply doesn't take time or make time for evangelism. Here is a personal experience to illustrate this point. For the last several years I have served on the local Board of Directors of Opportunities Industrialization Center (OIC). The chairman of the board of directors is Dr. Fred Sampson, an honored minister in the black community. In conversation with him we both agreed that this kind of ministry would render a two-fold service, as we understood life and religion. It would assist both blacks and whites who were either underemployed or unemployed to receive the necessary education and skill training that would enable them to secure jobs and thus become self-respecting, contributing members of society. In addition, we both agreed that we wanted to minister to the "whole" person, and this included spiritual needs. But I soon realized that while serving faithfully as a member of the board of directors, I had not spoken to even one person in this program about his relationship with Jesus Christ.

On the other hand it is possible to engage in social action as a means of evading the necessity of confronting an individual with his need for personal salvation. Again I quote a conversation with a fellow pastor. He said, "I find it increasingly difficult to talk to a person about his basic commitment to Christ. I see now that I have been engaging in social action as a means of evading this task. I would rather try to help someone in need, ten to one, than to speak to him about his relationship with God." Here is an honest confession. He is not alone.

For many of us it is not easy to lead a person to face the ultimate decision of life—who is to be God in my life? It is easy to find subtle and devious ways of avoiding it. Some use social service to give the "feeling" they are being religious, but in reality it is a "gimmick" used to salve their consciences because of the failure to confront the individual with Jesus Christ.

Those interested in evangelism are right in issuing a warning to us. We must listen and heed this warning. I have been critical of the failure of the church in the past. I must be equally critical of the "new" that seems to be emerging—if it is wrong. We must make sure that we are doing what God wants us to be doing. He is seeking redemption—total redemption. To be sure, this involves the physical and the social, but it also includes the spiritual. We are God's people, called to be instruments of redemption. This is what God is about, and it is what we must be about. Let's admit there is a temptation and a danger here, face it honestly, and overcome it.

3. Conclusion

Both extremes—advocates of evangelism and advocates of social involvement—have been so deeply committed to their particular emphases that it has been difficult for either even to listen to (much less to practice) the emphasis of the other. Erroneous and exaggerated statements, views, and actions abound on both sides and each has become excessively suspicious of the other, and has tended categorically to reject the other.

However, the difficulty is that each with its fear and rejection of the other is practicing and promoting an inadequate expression of the gospel because of an emphasis on *a part* of the gospel as though it were the whole. Each has a highly commendable commitment to a part of the gospel. Yet, each, by magnifying only a part, is guilty of perpetrating a tragic perversion of the gospel. It is true that serious errors can be pointed out on both extremes. These need to be identified and remedied. Then all of us can join together with zeal and commitment to practice the *whole* gospel.

The solution is not to be found simply in a toleration of one by the other or even a half-hearted acceptance of one by the other. We are not to take a little of one and a little of the other and seek to combine them. Rather we are to embrace both enthusiastically and wholly as essential and indispensable elements of the one gospel. We are not to "tip-toe" with reference to either emphasis. Neither is to receive simply a condescending "light touch." This was not the pattern of our Lord. With joyful abandon we are to go the limit with both emphases—to love God with our whole being and our neighbor as ourselves!

NOTES

1. To name a few: "All To Jesus, I Surrender," "Blessed Assurance, Jesus Is Mine," "Close to Thee," "O Safe to the Rock," "He Hideth My Soul in the Cleft of the Rock."

2. I am not antichurch though I have tried to write vigorously against institutionalism. I recognize both the importance and the necessity for the church as an institution and for organizations within the church through which certain essential aspects of the Christian faith are carried on.

3. Sherwood Eliot Wirt, *The Social Conscience of the Evangelical* (New York: Harper & Row, 1968), p. 152.

4. Stephen C. Rose, "Reformation or Revolution," Associated Press Syndication Service, 1968.

5. John Bright, *The Kingdom of God* (New York: Abingdon-Cokesbury, 1953), pp. 223–24.

6. Wirt, p. 9.

7. I am indebted to Edward Freeman for first introducing me to this information.

8. Timothy L. Smith, *Revivalism and Social Reform* (New York: Abingdon, 1957), p. 151.

9. Quoted in ibid., p. 225.

10. J. Wesley Bready, *This Freedom—Whence?* rev. ed. (New York: American Tract Society, 1942), p. 137.

11. Charles C. Cole, Jr., *The Social Ideas of the Northern Evangelists, 1826–1960* (New York: Columbia University Press, 1954), p. 97.

12. Ibid., p. 130. Cf. also pp. 102, 111.

13. Smith, p. 8.

14. Gerald I. Gingrich, *Protestant Revival Yesterday and Today* (New York: Exposition Press, 1969), p. 44.

15. J. Wesley Bready, *England: Before and After Wesley* (New York: Harper & Bro., n.d.), p. 226.

16. Ibid., pp. 228-29.

17. Smith, p. 223.

18. Quoted in Bready, p. 139.

19. Gingrich, p. 75.

20. Percy Livingstone Parker, ed., *The Heart of John Wesley's Journal* (London: Fleming H. Revell Co., n.d.), p. 206.

21. Quoted in Cole, p. 132.

22. Bready, pp. 245–46.

23. Ibid., p. 297.

24. Ibid., p. 252.

PART TWO

Practical Proposals

CHAPTER FIVE

Motivation for Mission

There is much evidence to indicate that the major religious expression of the average church member is to attend the Sunday morning worship service. Unfortunately there doesn't seem to be sufficient depth of commitment to motivate involvement in any serious way in a ministry for God in the world. To illustrate, one sensitive and serious church congregation appointed what they called a "renewal committee" to survey and give guidance to what they should do as "the People of God." After months of study the committee made a report to the church at a Sunday morning service. The report called attention to the fact that a small corps of people were expressing a ministry in the world. At the same time, with keen perception, the committee noted a weakness which points toward the basic problem in the life of today's churches. They called attention to those who criticize the church for not getting involved, not being relevant, and not getting where the action is. Yet, "when opportunities are pointed out where the church can get involved, and the call is extended to get on the firing line where the action is, far too few heed the call, and among those who are heedless to the call are those who are the most vocal in criticism." Then they drew the following conclusion: "Anyone who simply marks the failures of the church without giving himself and the best he has to correct those failures is not sincerely concerned about the failures, but is merely aware of them."

My own experience confirms this report. Time and again I hear people criticizing the church for its failure to become involved. They ask, "Why doesn't the church do something?" However, as a rule, they are not as willing to become involved as their words would indicate. When positive proposals and suggestions are made for action and involvement, the majority simply do not respond. They may be quite willing to attend a meeting in which they are "inspired," but to get involved is quite a different matter.[1]

Now, there are those who say that the renewal movement within the church has failed. They cite the fact that we have been talking about "renewal" for more than a decade; yet little by way of positive action has taken place. Many speeches have been made, conferences have been led, and books have been written. But the same few churches are constantly referred to as examples. In reality, the critics say, so far as church life in general is concerned, little has transpired.

The renewal movement has not failed. We have simply misunderstood what was needed for renewal to take place. It would seem that those who rediscovered and have been proclaiming the concept of "the ministry of the laity" concluded that once this concept was enunciated, everyone would "run over themselves" to get involved in this "ministry." As is altogether too obvious, this has not been the case. A few have caught the vision and have become involved, but the large majority of people in the churches are untouched and unmoved.

This does not mean that the concept of the ministry of the laity is erroneous, nor does it mean the renewal movement has failed. It simply means that we have misunderstood the nature of the problem we face. A part of the problem was related to understanding. The concept of the ministry of the laity had to be proclaimed so that understanding could take place. However, what we failed to realize adequately was that understanding was not all of the problem. Intelligent, deep, and serious commitment is also needed if involvement is to take place.

Thus we come to face the fact that the basic problem in the life of the church is a spiritual problem. We simply do not have the spiritual commitment we need to be an adequate expression of God's people in our time. Too many church members are committed half-heartedly to an institutionally oriented religion. While this results in a tenuous relationship with the church, it does not lead them to become involved with the world. Actually, it is relatively easy to talk about the "ministry of the laity" and the need for the laity to become "equipped for their ministry" and "involved in the world." But something of a *radical* nature must take place in the lives of most church members before they will be *willing* to accept their ministry and *willing* to become equipped and *motivated* to get involved. This is a spiritual problem, and only a spiritual experience will solve it.

This spiritual experience is not needed only by those outside the church or by those casual church members who are on the periphery of things. I am saying that *all*—those on the church staff, those in places of leadership, and those who constitute the core of the life of the church—all need to meet God at a deeper level of life. If we are going to be instruments of God which he can use to "turn on" the world, then first of all we must become "turned on."

POSSIBLE APPROACHES IN SEEKING PERSONAL RENEWAL

The question is, how will this spiritual experience "happen"? There is no *one* answer. This is the work of God and he works as he will. He cannot be ordered or manipulated. For some it may be a sudden, cataclysmic experience; for others it will be gradual. For some it may occur in the regular worship services; for others, in moments of private devotions. Many have had it happen in a retreat or conference, while others have found this personal spiritual awakening in a small group experience. Although God will not be "boxed" within a church program, there are some things which might be done to provide a "climate" in which the Holy Spirit may work. If I were pastor of a congregation, these are some of the things I would do in an effort to help people "come alive" at a deeper level in their spiritual experience.

1. *Preaching*

Preaching is one of the major and continuing means of leading people to understand and encounter God's call. I am aware that there are those who have rejected preaching as having any real or significant influence on the lives of people today. It may be true that in the past we tended to clothe the word spoken in the pulpit with an almost magical aura which was unrealistic. On the other hand, I am convinced that the preached word does carry weight with and have an influence on the lives of listeners.

Preaching, to be effective as I see it, must have a large element of teaching in it. The preacher's purpose should be to proclaim, with all the clarity possible, the nature of God's call and what it really means to be God's people. I would encourage the holding of "talk-back" sessions (or dialogue) after the sermons to give people the opportunity to ask questions, to challenge any statements made in the sermon, and to seek more information on the subject. As a preacher, I must realize that preaching is not a one-way street. Rather, it is a two-way street in which I proclaim, but the people must respond. At times the response will be verbal. But if this "new life" is to have any real significance for them, my listeners must discover it themselves! They must experience it. They must respond!

I believe preaching should be biblical but not dogmatic or authoritarian. This doesn't mean that I would not take advantage of and use the ideas and insights of others. But in attempting to learn what it really means to be the People of God, the Bible is the basic source of this information. It was to the Bible I turned for light and guidance.

In addition, I believe that preaching, on occasion, should be intensely personal. I would share my own search, my own struggles, failures, and discoveries. In doing this the preacher becomes exceedingly vulnerable. He runs the risk of destroying the symbol of perfection which some members unconsciously build up around him. Thus he becomes exposed as a human being with problems, weaknesses, and strivings. He confesses his humanity by sometimes having to say to people, "I don't know." But in becoming more personal and more human he becomes more real for the members. They will listen to him because they can identify with his struggles. He is searching as they are. Preaching that is personal is exceedingly important because of the need we all have for our religion to become personal and internalized!

2. *Personal Conversations*

None of these suggestions is unusual or startling. They are just some of the means by which I have observed things happen in the lives of people. Again, thinking from the perspective of the pastor, in my encounters with members in committee meetings, on the street, in homes, or otherwise, I would talk to them about their faith. So much of our conversions center on trivial matters. I would want to share some of my thinking with them and ask for their reaction. "I ran across an idea the other day and I would be interested in what you think about it." "There are those who say . . . How do you feel about it?" "Let me share with you an insight that I discovered recently. It has come to be very meaningful to me." There are, of course, occasions when our conversations should be light and breezy. On the other hand, there are times when our conversations ought to have substance to them.

This in-depth type of conversation should not be limited to pastor and member, but members will share with each other and with others. One of the characteristics of people who are beginning to have some deep and meaningful experiences with God is that they have a desire to share what they are discovering. So, over the telephone, in the home over a cup of coffee, in shops, in the office, in the grocery store, on the streets, the People of God will be engaged in animated conversation as one person shares with another what is happening in his life. One of the encouraging signs that is taking place today is that religion is beginning to be talked about in secular places.

3. *Reading Books*

Another characteristic of the renewal movement is the fact that people who are finding a deeper dimension in their Christian experience are reading, becoming excited about what they have read, and are sharing it with others. One of the things that was quite surprising to me in the early 1960s was the fact that the small group of people who had begun to be "turned on" in the church which I attend were actually reading books! And the books they were reading were stimulating and thoughtful. Actually, we were suggesting some of them for seminary students, and here were laymen carrying them around, reading them, and talking about them!

Happily, this is still going on. I rarely go to a conference or to a meeting that someone does not say to me, "Have you read . . .?"

Some excellent books are being written and published today. Therefore, one of the ways I would try to help people discover what God is seeking to do in the world and what he might do in their lives would be to suggest books which would be helpful. I would suggest that the church library purchase the best books available on personal and church renewal, and then I would encourage members to read them. Reference should be made from the pulpit to good books, and I would share titles with friends in personal conversations. Also, brief descriptions of certain books should appear in the church paper.

Elton Trueblood suggests that a church should make use of a "book table."[2] He believes that a church should set up a table with a large selection of books in a conspicuous and well-traveled location—and these books should be sold. Dr. Trueblood feels that if a person purchases a book he probably will read it with greater care, will mark it, and thus find it more meaningful. The person can also share the book with friends. He denounces vigorously the view that selling books in the church building is sacrilegious and says this is an "idolatry of bricks and mortar," which heresy Paul refuted in Acts 17:24. However one may feel about the validity of selling books in the church building, the basic point is still valid—namely, the reading and sharing of books is one means God is using today to help people make personal discoveries in their spiritual lives.

4. Retreats and Conferences

If I were a pastor seeking to provide both a climate and an opportunity in which Christians might meet God at increasingly deeper levels of their lives, I would make extensive use of retreats and conferences. Here I am not using the term "retreat" in its classical meaning in which all or a major portion of the experience is spent in silence. Rather, the term is used to denote those meetings that take place in a retreat setting—a place of withdrawal and quietness away from the bustle, noise, and activity of routine life. First, I would take advantage of some of the excellent national retreat centers and regional conferences that are presently available. Each center tends to have its own unique emphasis. One may emphasize personal, spiritual encounter; another may emphasize theological exploration in depth; another may emphasize psychological self-understanding; while another may emphasize involvement in the world. Therefore, it would be most important to understand the emphasis of a particular center so that you and your members would attend the one that met your own particular need.

Not everyone in the church will find these meetings helpful. Therefore, a pastor should exercise great care in inviting those who might attend such a conference or retreat. If I were a pastor, I would try to be sensitive as to whether the people who are invited would be "open" to what normally happens at a conference. As a rule, I would invite those who I had found to be "hurting," who were feeling the pains of disillusionment in their own lives and in what the church was doing. From a human (and perhaps selfish) viewpoint, I would urge those to attend who were held in esteem by the church and who had leadership responsibility. If in the future we felt basic changes needed to be made in the life of the church, these people would be helpful in leading others to recognize the validity of these changes.

The experience of a retreat or conference is valuable because it gives a person the opportunity to encounter his own "self" at a depth level which often is not present in the routine of life or in the regular services of the church. The retreat is a time of withdrawal— a time to get away from the demands of business and the constant ringing of the telephone. Here there is escape from the routine pressures that nag and pull in a hundred different directions.

Usually the retreat or conference center is located in a resort type of environment, thus affording, possibly, the opportunity to get out in the woods under God's sky and take a deep breath and look up. In this setting a person has both the opportunity and the stimulus to pause in the mad rush and reflect upon his life at a deeper level. He has the opportunity to ask, "Who, really, am I?" "Who is this that I have become?" "What am I doing with this existence I have?" "Is what I am doing the real meaning of what life is all about?" "Or am I being pushed by pressures into attitudes and actions which really are superficial?" It may be that all he has to do for a period of two or three days, or longer, is to think, to reflect. Also, there is usually the opportunity of sitting under excellent leaders, and there are others like him who are searching and with whom he can talk and pray. This kind of experience certainly affords the climate for encounter with self and with God which many have found to be transforming.

Because of the expense and distance involved in travel to these national and regional centers, the number from a given church who would be able to attend one of these retreats or conferences is limited. Therefore, I would urge that provision be made for retreat experiences for different groups within the church. This assumes, of course, that suitable facilities are available near the church. Overnight and weekend retreats for deacons, elders, and other official board members can be highly beneficial. Helpful retreat programs can also be provided for various leadership groups within the church, for couples, for the youth, for men, for women, etc. The important thing, I believe, is to provide an opportunity for as many as possible in the church to get away from the mad rush of life and have a chance for meaningful reflection and possible encounter.

5. *Lay Witness Weekend*

What appeals to one person may not at all appeal to another and what may be very meaningful in one church setting may "fall flat" in a different church setting. For this reason we must consider a variety of possible approaches. One that many churches have found to be very helpful is the lay witness weekend.[3]

This is an experience in which a group of laymen, who themselves have had an encounter with God in which new meaning has come into their lives, travel *at their own expense* to a particular church for a weekend to share with the people of that church. In forming the "team" a coordinator (a layman from another church) is selected, and he in turn is responsible for gathering others from various churches. The number selected is determined by the size of the church to be visited. The program, of course, may be varied, but there is a pattern which is usually followed. First, a general meeting is held at the church on Friday night. Preparation has been made to have as many of the adult membership present as possible. After a time of singing and fellowship, two or three of the visiting laymen share what has happened recently in their Christian lives. The large group then divides into smaller groups, each of which is led by a visiting layman. Again, opportunity is given for personal sharing.

On Saturday morning groups come together in the homes of various church members. Personal invitations have been issued previously to attend this Saturday morning "coffee." Again, under the leadership of a visiting layman there is a sharing of personal experiences. Additional meetings are held thoughout the day and evening. On Sunday morning the visiting laymen meet with the various adult classes, and in the morning worship service, one of the visitors gives his witness. On Sunday evening, after the visiting laymen have gone, the service is often open for a testimony meeting by the members of the church so they can share together the transforming experiences that have come out of the weekend. The pastors with whom I have talked who have had a lay witness weekend in their churches have been exceedingly enthusiastic in telling what this has meant in the lives of their members.

PERSONAL DISCOVERY THROUGH SMALL GROUPS

If I were a pastor, I would use all of the ideas mentioned so far (and others that I might find out about), but the major means I would use to help people "come alive" in their personal encounter with self and with God would be small groups—particularly "searching" groups.

During the last fifteen years the small group approach has burst forth into a movement. Without any organization to promote them, with little guidance except that which came from friend to friend, small groups have sprung up in a rather fantastic manner all over the nation and in other parts of the world. Evidently these groups are meeting a fundamental need in the lives of many people. It may be that in a world of depersonalization, groups enable the participants to discover more clearly their identity as persons. Or it may be that the group gives the individual a place where he can know and be known. It may be that the individual finds in the group a place where he no longer has to "fake it." In the group he can be his "real self" and know that he is accepted and loved as he is. Whatever the reasons, and undoubtedly they are numerous and complex, through experiences in a small group many people have found a new dimension in their Christian life. The testimony of Clyde Reid, who formerly was on the staff of the Institute for Advanced Pastoral Studies in Bloomfield Hills, Michigan, is typical.

> I have seen the lives of people change in small groups. I have seen people reborn in small groups. This is not using the word loosely, for individuals have gained a whole new foothold on life. My own life has been deeply affected and positively influenced by small groups, and my wife would tell you the same. I have seen people gain exciting new insights. I have seen them grow in self-confidence and self-acceptance, and I have seen persons come to know who they really are for the first time in their lives.[4]

Before we take a look at the practical aspects of the small group, there are some preliminary matters that need to be noted briefly. First, small groups do not appeal to everyone. People are different and there are those for whom the small group would hold neither interest nor meaning. This does not mean they are more or less dedicated or more or less mature than others. It simply means that personalities are different, experiences have been different, and thus needs and interests are different. This says two things. First, we should not try to get everyone in a small group. Second, we should not "sit in judgment" on those who are not a part of a small group.

In the second place, it must be admitted that there are potential dangers in small groups. Some pastors and church leaders have had such a negative experience that they feel such groups are a serious threat to the church. There are even some pastors who feel that small groups are the work of Satan and must be resisted at all costs. As one pastor stated it, "If ever there are small groups in this church it will be over my dead body."

Let's examine some of the reasons for a negative attitude toward small groups. Some small groups have turned into torrid gossip sessions of criticism of the local church. They become antichurch and antipreacher. One reason these groups come into formation in the first place is that there is a certain amount of disillusionment with what the church is doing. Thus the temptation is very real for the participants to voice their frustrations concerning the failures of the church as they see them. Often the pastor comes in for his share of the criticism. Sometimes the members of the group have been led to leave the church completely. If this is what the small group is and does, no wonder the pastor condemns it. No pastor is going to look with favor on groups that are going to become bastions of opposition and criticism. This is a danger that must be vigorously avoided.

Still another danger is that a group may get under the domination of a person with a powerful personality, and the group may be led off on a tangent theologically. A third danger is that the group may try to be amateur psychiatrists. In their attempt to be "open" and "honest" they may tear a person apart and not be able to put him together again. The group may become introvert, with their concerns always turned inward. Recognizing the potential dangers involved, however, the small group is one approach to deep, personal discovery. If I were pastor in a local church, I not only would permit small groups, I would encourage them! The potential for good in small groups far outweighs the potential dangers.

There are many different types of small groups. Therefore it is extremely important that a person carefully identify the type of group he desires to join. Otherwise he may be looking for one type of experience, and the group with which he unites may have quite a different purpose. In such a situation it is quite likely that the individual will be disappointed and his needs not be met.

Groups devoted to Bible study are among the most popular. These are usually made up of people who for one reason or another have not found the Bible study in their particular church to be satisfying, and they meet during the week in someone's home to "study the Bible."

The prayer group differs from the Bible study group, though they may sometimes study the Bible. Usually these are people who have a deep belief in and commitment to intercessory prayer, and this is the primary purpose that draws them together. They meet to share their common concerns and spend the major portion of their time together in prayer. The prayer therapy group was made popular by Dr. William R. Parker.[5] Their emphasis is to seek to understand self better from a psychological perspective and to make one's personality weakness a matter of prayer and work. Each individual in the group takes a personality test which is analyzed by Dr. Parker and his staff. The interpretation is then sent to each person. If the person so desires he may share this interpretation with the group. It is then discussed by the group and made a matter of prayer and work by the individual.

Evangelistic or witnessing groups have been espoused primarily by Claxton Monro, an Episcopalian rector from Houston, Texas. Recognizing that it is becoming increasingly difficult to get nonchurch members to come to the church building, Monro started having evangelistic groups to meet monthly in various homes in his parish. The approach used in these groups is as follows. Two people are carefully chosen who are to give their witness. One is to share briefly and simply how he met Christ in a saving experience. The other is to share some area in which God is working in his life now. Church members invite their nonchurch friends to go with them to these meetings. The guests are told what kind of meeting it is going to be. There is no attempt to get people there by deceptive or devious means. Monro's testimony is that in this informal setting, with this simple, personal sharing, many have "come alive" in Christ.[6]

Vocational groups of many varieties exist. There are groups of doctors who meet each week in hospitals to share and pray. Other professional and business men have a weekly meeting during lunch. Factory workers have a similar meeting during their lunch period.

There are also mission groups. These are people who are committed to fulfilling some mission for God somewhere in his world. The mission group will be discussed in detail in the next chapter.

PRACTICAL SUGGESTIONS FOR A SEARCHING GROUP

The different types of groups mentioned above are fine, and each in its own way ministers to the needs of people. However there is another type of group that meets the special need of certain individuals at a particular point in their spiritual development. It is the single most effective means I know to enable people to find this "new life," this deeper relationship and commitment to the living God which is basic to any "renewed" church. I call this a "searching group."[7]

1. *Nature and Purpose*

It is important that we understand the nature and purpose of this type of group. A searching group is composed of people who, at a significant level in their lives, are searching for a deeper reality of God. As I have sought to analyze these who find this experience meaningful, it seems that two characteristics are common (though there are exceptions). First, they have either a deep sense of disillusionment about the church or a significant feeling of personal emptiness in their spiritual lives or both. These are people who have met God. Quite often they are leaders in the institutional church. Many have taught in Sunday school, or they have worked with women's groups or with men. Some have served on the official board of their church. But somehow all this activity has come to lose its meaning. They have a feeling of emptiness, or meaninglessness. This is the negative aspect of their feeling. There is also a positive aspect which is the second characteristic of these people. Although there is this feeling of spiritual emptiness (the intensity of this differs with different people), they also have a deep desire to discover that reality which does give meaning. They are convinced that there is a deeper meaning both to religion and to life than they have discovered up to this point. And these people want so deeply to find this reality and meaning that they are willing to engage in whatever search is necessary to make this discovery.

Both characteristics are important. For example, if a person were to become a part of a searching group and he had not experienced any sense of disillusionment, when the others began to share their frustrations and hang-ups, he probably wouldn't be able to understand what was happening. A person has to "hurt" before he will be willing to search at the level necessary for meaningful answers in a searching group. On the other hand, there are those who "ache" but are no longer sure that there is any reality within the institutional church. These often leave the church. Their reaction is to "chuck" the whole thing. Unfortunately, they are not usually interested in becoming part of a group "on search."

Thus the one who is committed to the reality of God yet does not have a sense of "ache" will usually fail to find a searching group meaningful. The one who "aches" but who is not committed to discover this reality at a deeper level of his life will not engage in the search. Both *ache* and *commitment to search* are essential for those who become part of a searching group.

This is not a "confession" group in which the participants gather each week and confess all their sins of the present and past. Confession is a most wholesome and helpful experience when it is properly understood and engaged in. But, unfortunately, some groups have made their shared experience a time when they dig up all the trash in their lives and seemingly enjoy reliving past sins. It is important to realize that a person may dig too deeply into some phase of his life and be hurt rather than helped.

The basic purpose of the searching group is to probe for a deeper meaning in religion and life which one has not yet discovered. It is a search to discover a deeper reality of God in life. This is a group in which one shares his frustrations, questions, and doubts. Concerned individuals share their searching and struggle to find more fullness and meaning in their own lives. They also share their searching and struggle to become the kind of person who genuinely loves and cares for other people. It is this kind of person God is seeking to help his people become. And to become God's person is the deep desire of their life. These are people who are confident that in such a meeting the Holy Spirit will be present to minister and to transform.

2. *Size of Group*

Groups may be of different sizes, depending on their purpose. For example, a Bible study or a prayer group may be relatively large (twenty to twenty-five persons). A searching group should be limited to between six and ten. Eight seems to be ideal. If it grows to twelve in number, it would be wise to consider dividing into two groups. The searching group must be small enough so that each person has a feeling of significance, yet large enough for dynamic interchange. Every person must be able to speak and be spoken to in each meeting. When the group becomes large, it is easy for the aggressive persons to dominate and for the shy ones to withdraw. If this is to be a personal sharing or searching group, then each person must open his life to be ministered to by the group.

3. *How to Start a Searching Group*

There is no one pattern that should be followed in starting a small group. What follows is only a suggestion because each group must find its own way if it is to be meaningful and alive. Here I want to share the pattern of the first group of which I was a part.

It was about 1960, and as far as I can remember, I had never heard of "small groups." This was the period in my life when I was going through an experience of severe disillusionment with the church. Then one Sunday I heard someone mention somthing about a "group" in our church.

If I remember correctly, this group was referred to in derision. However, my curiosity was pricked, and I did some investigating. I found that they came into existence quite spontaneously—almost by accident. It was started by our minister of education and a few of the young adults in the church. Over a period of time I observed their lives. They were not "kooks." In fact they were a part of the core leadership in the life of our church. There was a deacon and his wife, a couple were Sunday school teachers, and one or two were leaders in the church training program. Two of the ladies held leadership positions in the women's work. I had known all of them for years. They were good, solid church members—among the best we had. Yet, as I observed these people and began to talk to them, they seemed to have a freshness and "aliveness" that I had not known before. Religion which before had been prosaic and routine suddenly had become exciting to them. I noted also that a unique bond of relationship seemed to have grown up among them. They seemed to love one another. I had heard about "love one another" in sermons. But now for the first time, I think, I was witnessing it—and it was startling. Lest I give the impression that the group was a "clique," let me hasten to add that these people also seemed to love other people in a way that was different.

So, I went to the minister of education and shared with him my sense of disillusionment concerning the church and the spiritual poverty I felt in my own life. When I told him I wanted to join the group, he replied, "No, our group is large enough. You start your own group." This shook me. In the first place I had never tried to join anything before in my church when they wouldn't let me do it. Also I didn't know a thing about starting or conducting a group. When I protested, he said that if I would get a group together someone from their group would meet with us to share their experiences.

We now had the first essential for starting a searching group—one person who wants it desperately. How was I to go about trying to find participants for the group? My minister of education gave me only one statement for guidance. This is the second essential. He said, "You find some other people who 'ache' like you do."[8] I didn't fully understand what he meant until I had a chance to reflect upon it in the days immediately ahead. Then I set out to find some of these people. In talking with friends and acquaintances, I would get around as soon as possible to saying something "religious," and then I would listen to their reply. If they sounded like they "ached," I would probe more deeply. I wanted to find how deep their "ache" was. There are a lot of people who "hurt" a little. They don't like the hymns that are sung, or they do not like the time a certain meeting is held, but their hurt has not grabbed their insides. I was looking for people who ached to the bottom of their feet. Finally I found seven other people besides myself and we started with nine—one from the other group.

4. *When and Where to Meet*

These groups may meet any time, anywhere. Time and place should be determined by the convenience and desire of the members. There are those who feel that a home provides a more relaxed and informal setting for this type of sharing. If the meetings are held in the home, provision must be made to care for the children (when not in school or those too young for school). On the other hand, meeting at the church has its advantages. Since the church of which I am a member has a church training program on Sunday night, our group decided this was the best time and place for us to meet. This also meant that our children were cared for because they participated in the church training program for their age group. Also meeting at this time made it possible for both men and women to participate.

Many groups composed entirely of women meet during the morning hours while their older children are at school. A baby-sitter is usually secured to care for the smaller children. As a rule, men's groups meet during an early morning hour or at the lunch hour. Mixed groups will need to meet after work hours, in the evening or on weekends.

5. *The First Few Meetings*

What is the group to do the first few times it meets? These first meetings are quite crucial because they tend to set the "tone" of what may follow. Yet this is the time when the group has little or no experience in what to do. It may be helpful to obtain some printed materials to serve as guidelines for getting started.[9]

However, in the group of which I was a part, when we met for the first time, we decided that we needed to get to know each other better. Having been members of the same church for a number of years, we knew each other by name though none of us happened to be friends socially. So we decided that each person in the group would do two things: (1) Share his conversion experience, and (2) Tell why he felt the need for a group such as this. I thought all nine of us could easily do this in the one hour to which our meeting was limited. But it took us six weeks to get around to everyone! Some of them, who previously had seemed quite ordinary, shared some thrilling experiences centered around their encounter with Christ. There were times when we came close to having a revival. At other times we shared in despair as a member would tell of the dull routine in his church life in recent years and the growing emptiness and meaninglessness of it all.

In the sharing of these experiences, some joyful and some agonizing, we began to develop a bond—an understanding of each other and a caring for each other—that was to be the central characteristic of our group.

6. *Disciplines*

It is imperative for a searching group to live its shared life under certain disciplines. Disciplines in our context were certain things which each member of the group covenants with the others to observe. These group covenants are kept with utmost seriousness. Each group is completely free to choose whatever disciplines they want to follow. There is no one set of disciplines, but it is important that the group demonstrate the seriousness of their purpose by selecting certain disciplines under which their lives together will be lived. No one in our group was on the staff of the church. I was the only ordained clergyman. Thus no one's "job" in the church was in any way threatened. So from the very beginning we were able to talk to each other about the disciplines in a very frank and open manner. The five chosen by our group were as follows.

(1) *The Discipline of Attendance.* We agreed that this was not a

regularly scheduled church meeting which a person ought to attend from a sense of obligation. It was understood that we were meeting together, not because we ought to, but because we had to. There was an ache in our lives, and we wanted to join with others who were serious in their search for something (we didn't know what to call it) that would give a deeper meaning to our lives. We agreed that if a person did not feel deeply about the meeting and if he or she was unwilling to commit himself or herself seriously to the group, then this ought to be admitted at the outset, and the individual should withdraw. Also it was clearly understood that if anyone came to feel that the group was not meeting a need in his life, he was perfectly free to withdraw. Our covenant was that we would agree to be present at every meeting unless providentially hindered.

(2) *The Discipline of Prayer.* Our second discipline was that we would covenant with each other to pray daily, by name, for each member of the group. Since there were nine of us, this meant that each of us would pray by name each day for the eight other members. It was not to be the usual type of prayer that is so typical of many of us . . . we get in the bed at night, tired and sleepy, and then remember that we have not done our praying for that day. So very quickly we rush through the routine, "God bless Bill; God bless Sam; God bless Mary; God bless Susie, etc." We agreed that we would not be content with the "God bless . . ." type of prayer.

We came to know each other in such fashion that each day we would lift the others before God in the area of his particular struggle. For example, one of the members of our group worked for a large industrial plant in Louisville. A plant foreman with whom he was rather closely related in work was an alcoholic. His wife was also an alcoholic. My friend's deepest concern in life at that particular time was to be a witness and a minister to this man and his wife. I can remember many a time praying a prayer something like the following: "God be with ———— this week. On the job help him to *be* the kind of person that will encourage this man to talk with him. And if he does, give ———— the kind of guidance he needs to know what to do and what to say." I recall being so caught up in this prayer that many times before our meeting would begin, I would have to check with ———— to see what, if anything, had happened during the week.

Another group member was a mother who had a retarded child. Again I can remember praying something like: "God be with

——————— today. Help her to have the patience and understanding to know how to relate properly to her child. Also help her to know how to relate to the other children in the family—and be with the other children as they relate to this child. I confess I don't understand this, nor do I know how I would react in this type of situation. Help me to give ——————— the support she needs."

One thing further needs to be noted in connection with the discipline of daily prayer. A person cannot pray for people like this every day, calling them by name and lifting them to God in the area of their struggle, without coming to love them deeply. Actually, my love for them became much deeper than the relationship I have with some of my best friends socially. We came to know each other and to care for each other on a deeper level.

(3) *The Discipline of Study.* We agreed that our search was not going to be a glorified "bull session." It is true that our sharing was going to be primarily personal, however, we felt the need of something to guide us in our search. Therefore, we covenanted together that we would accept the discipline of study. There are at least three major resources available for this study. First, a group may decide to study some book of the Bible. The question then arises, what is the difference in this type of group studying the Bible and a Bible study group? The difference is the way in which the Bible is studied. A Bible study group certainly seeks to make their teaching relevant to the lives of the members. However, the emphasis is on the teachings and meaning of the Bible. In a searching group the emphasis is different. While this group is concerned with the proper understanding of the teachings and meaning of the Bible, the central thrust is always personal. For example, in a study of a passage on forgiveness, the Bible group would tend to come out with something like this: "It seems to me the meaning is so and so." In a searching group the discussion would center around something like this: "To be perfectly honest, my real struggle in this area is ———————."

A second area of resources that is available for guiding the study of the group is the great devotional classics.[10] In sharing the struggles of the great Christians of the past, we find guidance for life today.

Another source for study and discussion is to be found in the excellent books that are currently being written in the area of renewal. Books by Keith Miller, Elton Trueblood, Elizabeth O'Connor, Lyman Coleman, Bruce Larson, Ralph Osborne, and others have been used by many with great profit.

Again, attention must be called to the fact that the study of these devotional classics or renewal books must be intensely personal. A great temptation the group faces is to make their study *conceptual* rather than *personal*. That is, they study the book to see what the book says. They discuss the *ideas* presented. Of course, they give their reaction to these ideas, but this is not what I mean by being personal. There is a tendency for the group to react as follows: "One of the ideas I like best is ——————." Or, "One place where I really agree with him is ——————." Here the group is still dealing with concepts or ideas. What they ought to be saying is something like this: "My problem in this area is ——————." Or, "Last week I ——————." When the group becomes conceptual they are avoiding being personal.

Each member of our group committed himself to the discipline that he would fulfill the assigned study each week. Since we had no one who was the "teacher," this was very important. Each person was equal and thus equally responsible for contributing to the group, sharing his personal struggles in the area with which the study dealt. If one of the members of the group had said, "I am so terribly busy I simply do not have the time to study, but I would like to come to your meetings and listen to you talk," our response would have been, "We would like very much to have you as a part of our group—if you can accept and meet our disciplines, however, if you cannot we are very sorry. We are completely serious about our search and cannot have anyone sitting on the sidelines 'listening to us talk.'"

(4) *The Discipline of Confidentiality.* So far as the searching group is concerned (this may or may not be true for a Bible study group or a prayer group) the discipline of confidentiality is indispensable. Without the sense of trust which is built on confidentiality, it cannot become a searching group but would simply end up by being an interesting conversational gathering.

Our group covenanted together that we would keep everything that was said in our meetings in the strictest of confidence. We agreed that we would not repeat anything that was said in the group to any other person outside the group at any time in any place. There was one man in the group whose wife was not a member of the group. It was agreed that he would not tell his wife anything that was said.

However, although we all agreed on this discipline of confidentiality, it was some weeks before we began building a relationship of trust. The matter of trust is not something which a group can legislate. It is a matter of relationship and is built on experience. So in starting

our study and sharing together, we began with those things that were
relatively shallow and on the surface of our lives. After we had been
meeting for a number of weeks, one Sunday night one of the members opened his life at a deeper level. We could almost feel the tension
as each one waited to see how the others were going to respond to
this openness. When the group reached out to him with genuine love,
care, and concern, then another person dared to open his life at a bit
deeper level. After a period of months we came to the place where we
loved one another so much and trusted each other so much we were
sharing problems, questions, doubts, and struggles that had long been
buried because of embarrassment or fear.

The question is often raised, "Why can't we use our present church
structures (Sunday school classes, training groups, or other groups) to
become this type of small group?" My own feeling is that this is not
possible.[11] Let me give a hypothetical illustration to indicate why I
have come to this conclusion. I have been a member of a men's Sunday school class in my church for several years. We know each other
well and have developed a close fellowship. On Sunday morning we
greet each other, "Hi, Bill! Hi, Joe! Hi, Findley!" Suppose my wife
and I are having some major difficulties, and one Sunday morning in
the class I say, "Fellows, I'm having some real trouble at home. My
wife and I are fighting all the time. All day long, it's nag, nag, nag.
That's the first thing I hear when I get up in the morning. When I
come home from work, she takes it up again without missing a beat.
Every time I open my mouth, she puts her foot in it. One night last
week we had a real 'set to.' I tell you I don't know whether I can
stand much more of this or not. I've just about had it! If this keeps
up I just don't see anything for us but divorce." If I were to say this
in my Sunday school class, do you think those men would make this
a matter of prayer, love, and concern for me? Would they keep it in
strictest confidence? You know they wouldn't! The church foyer
would be alive with buzzing, "Have you heard about ol' Edge and
his wife? Yeah, man, they are fighting all the time. I heard they had
a fight last week and he knocked her down!" It would be all over the
church before twelve o'clock.

I know that would happen, so what do I do when I come to Sunday
school? Someone says to me, "How are you doing, Findley?" I reply,
"Fine, couldn't be better." The fact is, I may be boiling inside. I may
have problems with my job or with my teenage children that are
nearly eating my insides out. But I'm not going to let them know

about it. When they ask, "How're you doing?" my reply is always, "Fine! Fine!"

It is possible that it is in church where we are most dishonest! We play a role calculated to make others see us as we want them to . . . everything under control . . . no problems. We want them to think that we never have any doubts about the Bible or the Christian faith, that our faith is perfect and is unwavering. Every effort is made to get across the idea that we never have any difficulties on the job. Our relationship with the boss is always perfect, and there are no problems with anyone in the office. We want them to think that we never have any family problems. Our relationship with our spouse is just great, and we never have any problems with the children. Our teenage children never cause a minute's anxiety. They are always home at the appropriate hour. We don't want them to know that there are times when we have self-doubts and ache with a hundred problems and questions. No, at church we want everyone to think that "for me and my house" I've got everything under control.

But this is not the reality of my life. I do have problems at the office. I do have problems at home, with my children, with my faith. And I need a group of people with whom I can be *me!* The title of the rock song, "I Gotta Be Me," has a basic message in it. I need a place where, to whatever extent I want to, I can uncover the real me—with all my humanity, my weakness, my problems, my questions —and know that in spite of this—no, because of this—I will be loved and accepted. And I can know that everything is held in the strictest confidence.

Now we come to the essence of this trust relationship. Our group started out by agreeing that we would hold all matters in confidence. But we did not really trust each other because we didn't know each other well enough. But in time, as we shared, struggled, laughed, wept, and prayed together we came to love each other at a depth level that was unique in my Christian experience (though I had been in the professional Christian ministry for years). As I reflect on that experience, the real reason I would not say anything that would hurt one of the members of the group had nothing to do with the fact that months before we had accepted a discipline of confidentiality. The real reason was that I cared for them too deeply.

It was in this experience that I came to understand more deeply and more clearly the meaning of *agape*—Christian love. We all tend to talk glibly about "loving one another." I had talked about it, taught

about it, and I had preached on it, but I had never really experienced
it until I became a part of this group. Here I came to know what it
meant to care and to be cared for, to love and to be loved. My ability
to care for and love others for God was deepened because I was cared
for and loved by this group.

(5) *The Discipline of Sharing.* There was something which we did
agree we could and would share. We would not share what was said
in the group, but if God began to work in our lives in a meaningful
way and if we felt any change was taking place in our lives, we would
share it with others. We would also seek to be a caring person for God,
thus fulfilling a "general mission" through a caring ministry in our
everyday relationships.

7. Questions Frequently Asked

In discussing small groups with people in churches as well as with
students in the classroom, there are a number of questions that are
asked repeatedly. Perhaps it would be helpful to consider some of
these. However, there is such variety and flexibility to small groups
that to attempt to tell "how it ought to be done" is really an impossible task.

What procedure is followed during the meeting? Some groups that
meet in homes have a brief time for informal fellowship. This needs
to be guarded carefully, however. The temptation may be to have only
informal fellowship and not get down to serious searching. In the first
group of which I was a part, there were three divisions to our meeting. First, we began with ten minutes of silence. Since we were meeting in a room in the church, we agreed that when each person opened
the door he would immediately observe silence. Our chairs were in a
circle, and when a person came, if there were others already in the
room, there were no greetings. He would simply come in and take a
seat in silence. Each person would bring a Bible or devotional book
with him if he so desired. These ten minutes we would spend reading
the Bible, praying, and meditating. We used this as a means for each
person to try to gather himself together and to focus in on God.

An appointed person would call an end to the silence and we would
begin the second part of the meeting—discussion and sharing. This
took up most of our time together. Third, we would conclude the

meeting with prayer. This we sought to do in a variety of ways. Many have found conversational prayer to be quite meaningful in this context.[12]

Does the group have a leader? Ours did not. Although the members of our group had quite differing educational backgrounds, everyone assumed equal responsibility. No one felt he had to be "teacher." This was most fortunate. Each week we did appoint someone to be "leader" for the next week, but the only responsibility he had was to check his watch and tell the group when it was time to break the silence. He would also initiate the discussion. But once the discussion began he had no more responsibility than anyone else in the group. At the end of the session he would appoint someone else to be "leader" for the next week.

How long should each meeting last? This varies widely. Actually each group will have to find what is best for them. Some groups meet up to three hours with a coffee break somewhere near midpoint. Others meet for two hours with a time of informal fellowship following. Ours met for one hour, but this was primarily because we had to fit into the schedule of the church. It is important to meet long enough so that meaningful searching and sharing has time to emerge. On the other hand the meeting should not be so long that it tends to become a drag. If I were to express a preference as to time, I would say an hour and a half.

Should a husband and wife be in the same group? All other things being equal my answer would be, "Yes." This assumes, of course, that both of them want to be in a group, that is, that each has both the ache and the yearning. If God begins to work in the group and if something meaningful begins to happen, it is better for the husband and wife to share this experience together. Also, when they are in the same group they can talk at home (alone) about the things that were discussed in the group. This means that the sharing continues throughout the week, not just during the meeting.

A few years ago my answer to this question would have been an unequivocal "Yes." However, an experience I had changed my mind. There was a young couple whom I knew were participating in separate small groups. On inquiring as to why this was the case, the wife replied, "When I am in a group with my husband, I feel intimidated. I tend to 'clam up.'" (This was quite a surprise to me. Though I thought I knew her, I never suspected this.) She continued, "When he is not present I feel so free I just babble on like a brook." If this is the situation with either the husband or wife, they ought to be in different groups.

Should the pastor be in a group? This depends on the pastor and on the group. There are some pastors who feel so deeply about their symbolic role as minister that they believe it would be unwise to open their lives and share with any of their members on this level. This is a point that needs to be considered. Other pastors feel that it is possible for them to share their lives as human beings with certain members of their congregation. A totally different difficulty a pastor has in being a part of a searching group is the tendency he has to dominate and the tendency of the laymen to submit. Strange though it may seem, it is not an easy thing for a pastor to be a human being in a group that is discussing religious problems. All his background and training tend to set him up as the authority. When the laymen have said all they know about the problem, they turn to him for "the answer." Obviously this type of person would be a serious detriment to a group. It should be said, however, that many pastors can be "human beings," and they have found rich and meaningful experiences in groups with certain of their church members. In some larger churches, members of the church staff have formed themselves into a searching group and found a deeply meaningful experience.

Should new people be permitted to join a group? This is a difficult question. (Not because it is difficult to know what seems to be the right answer but because the right answer seems to be harsh.) First, let's look at some of the facets of the problem before suggesting a possible answer. If the members of the group are finding the experience meaningful, it is only natural that they share with their friends what is happening (the fifth discipline). It would also be only natural for some of these friends to say that they, too, have this frustration and gnawing ache in their spiritual lives and indicate they would like to be a part of this group. Certainly we would want our friends to share in an experience that is so meaningful. We don't want to be an exclusive clique! So, our natural response is, "Of course, let new people come in the group!"

But there is a problem. Suppose the group has been meeting for six months and a significant degree of trust relationship has been built among the participants. Then someone brings a friend to the group. This changes the whole climate. They don't know this new person and are not sure whether they can trust him (or her). So for that meeting the group reverts to where they were near the beginning and talks about things that are relatively superficial. When after a couple of months this person is assimilated and another new person is brought in, the same thing happens again. If a new person is brought in each month, the group tends to develop only a one month level of trust.[13]

What, then, is a solution? On the one hand, we want all the people who desire this kind of experience to have it. We don't want to be exclusive and insensitive to the desires and needs of others. This is certainly not Christian. On the other hand, if the group keeps bringing in new people the level of trust relationship which is essential to the purpose and functioning of the group cannot be achieved. The best answer I have found so far is that once the group begins to develop trust relationships, do not let new members in. What about the other people who need and want this experience? Start a new group for them with a person, or couple, from the first group meeting with them. This one (or couple) can continue to meet with his original group too if he so desires.

There are two related questions that grow out of the above discussion. Once the word gets around that there are groups meeting in the church (and homes) where they will not let any new members join, there will be a strong tendency on the part of the others to think of them as "exclusive cliques" and "a bunch of Holy Joes." How can this be either avoided or minimized? Closely related to this is the question, how can we make this experience available to all church members who desire it without trying to "promote" small groups. To "promote" small groups as we have tried to promote the regular church program would be an unfortunate thing. A small group, in a sense, ought to be a "happening." It ought to come into existence, not because it was promoted, but because the Holy Spirit was working in the lives of some people. Thus the problem is: How might a church provide the opportunity and the climate in which groups may be born without the pressure of promotion?

The charge of exclusivism can be eliminated by letting the total church membership know that this experience is available for everyone. One church met the situation in this manner. Adequate publicity was given to the announcement that on a certain Wednesday night during the regular prayer meeting hour there would be a meeting for all the people who were interested in being a part of a one-month small group experiment. At the appointed time each person was given a card on which he wrote his name, address, and telephone number.

Each was also asked to check his first, second, and third choices as to the time he would like for his small group to meet, i.e., Monday morning, Monday afternoon, Monday night, Tuesday morning, Tuesday afternoon, etc. The church staff then took the cards and made a list of all the groups in terms of their preferred time of meeting.

The people were asked to be back the next Wednesday night. At this time the lists were passed out so that everyone would know who was in their group. They then went to a different room for their organizational meeting. The church staff had prepared and passed out mimeographed resource materials which could be used to guide their daily meditation and their weekly meeting. It was clearly understood that the experiment was to last for one month only. If, at the end of that time, anyone had not found the experience profitable, the experiment was concluded. If, on the other hand, one had found the experience meaningful and desired to continue in a small group experience, he could so indicate this to the church staff and they would see that he was put in touch with others who also desired this experience. Thus no one could say this was only for an exclusive "bunch of Holy Joes." Also it made the experience available for all without pressure of any kind.

How can the group be prevented from becoming critical of the church? This, of course, is one of the major criticisms some pastors have of these groups. It must be admitted that there are some groups where "what's wrong with the church" and "what's wrong with the preacher" is the basic thrust. If this happens, it is most unfortunate not only for the church but also for the group because this is certainly not the basic purpose. Yet, we have admitted that a certain amount of frustration and a certain ache is characteristic of people who become participants in a searching group. How can we keep this frustration and criticism from being directed toward the church? A good principle for the group to adopt (it might be a sixth discipline) is as follows: We agree not to discuss any problem unless we begin the statement of it with the personal pronoun, "I" or "my." This keeps the group from talking about "them" or "they." Incidentally, using the pronoun "I" or "my" helps keep the discussion personal, as it ought to be, rather than letting it become conceptual.

How long should a searching group keep in existence? This, too, is difficult to answer. Some groups have been going for years and are still dynamic and vital. On the other hand, some suggest that the group ought to set a time limit of six months when they first get started. If at that time the participants feel that the group is really not doing anything for them, it can die an honorable death. On the other hand if they are finding it helpful, they can decide to go on for another six months.

This raises another question. Should a searching group go on indefinitely? "No!" As mentioned earlier, one of the criticisms of small groups is that they tend to become as introverted as any organization we have in the church. This is a danger that must be faced frankly by every searching group. When the experience of the searching group is positive, the members do come to care for one another deeply. They find their lives becoming increasingly intertwined as they share and pray together, and they are thrilled as they feel hope and new life surging within them. With the glow of these experiences the temptation for the group is to "build a tabernacle" and stay on the mountaintop. If this happens, there may well be justification to the criticism that they are simply "navel gazing" and "feeding off one another."

The purpose of the searching group must again be brought clearly into focus. It is to help individuals to discover a new life in God and a deeper relationship with him. This is basic; but it is not the whole of the Christian experience, but only a first step. The purpose of the Christian's life is to be on mission for God in the redemption (personal and social) of his world. The purpose of the searching group is to help people find this "new life," but it is also concerned with getting us ready to go out on mission for God.

If these people do not find and express some ministry for God somewhere in his world, they have misunderstood the nature of the Christian life and the purpose of the searching group. Now to answer the question. The searching group is not to remain in existence indefinitely. It is successful when it dies, that is, when its members, one at a time, come to discover their mission in the world and leave to join a mission group.

NOTES

1. I am not here placing all the blame on the laity for the failure of the church to become involved. The responsibility must rest upon the shoulders of the clergy who are largely responsible for teaching the laymen to be what

they now are. Then, behind the clergy, the responsibility must rest upon the seminaries who taught the clergy to be what they now are.

2. Elton Trueblood, *The Incendiary Fellowship* (New York: Harper & Row, 1967), p. 63.

3. For information, write to The Institute of Church Renewal, 1610 La-Vista Road, N.E., Atlanta, Ga., 30329.

4. Clyde Reid, *Groups Alive—Church Alive* (New York: Harper & Row, 1969), p. 11.

5. William R. Parker and Elaine St. Johns, *Prayer Can Change Your Life* (Englewood Cliffs, N. J.: Prentice-Hall), 1957.

6. Claxton Monro and William S. Taegel, *Witnessing Laymen Make Living Churches* (Waco, Tex.: Word Books, 1968).

7. These groups are also called "personal groups," "struggling groups," "growth groups," etc.

8. There will be those who feel that "aching" is not essential for a person to be part of a searching group—and they may be right. I certainly do not want to be dogmatic at this point. The only thing I would say is there must be something in the life of the individual that will motivate him to search on the depth level that is necessary to make a searching group meaningful. Need and motive—both must be deep.

9. See Appendix.

10. For an excellent introduction to some of the devotional classics from a historical perspective, see E. Glenn Hinson, *Seekers after Mature Faith* (Waco, Tex.: Word Books, 1968).

11. There have been a few who said they had a class or some other church group that achieved this type of trust relationship but this is rare.

12. For an explanation of conversational prayer, see Rosalind Rinker, *Prayer: Conversing With God* (Grand Rapids: Zondervan, 1959).

13. This is one reason it is not possible for our present church organizations whose purpose is to bring in new people to become this kind of group.

CHAPTER SIX

A Practical Program for Mission

L et those be warned who, in their haste to find some practical suggestions, turn first to this section to try to find a "practical program" and omit a careful consideration of the theological and personal bases which precede. This would be a tragic mistake, for renewal in its essence is the gift of God. It is the work of the Holy Spirit. It is a meeting with God at a deeper level of one's life. No practical program can substitute for this "happening" in the individual's life. It is here renewal must begin. To approach it in any other way is to seek to create it through institutional or promotional technique.

However, if renewal is to be anything more than an individual "happening," if in any sense it is a corporate experience, if it is going to conserve some values that have been discovered, and if the attempt is going to be made to communicate these values to others, then renewal must have some form. Here we come face to face with the ever present problem of the potential conflict between freedom and form, between institutions and institutionalism.

To try to "program" renewal is the last thing I would want to do. This would be contrary to everything I have tried to say about the institutionalization of the modern church.[1] To present practical suggestions or possible proposals for a new approach may be the first step in a new institutionalism. Nevertheless, this is a danger that must be run and a risk that must be taken. The problem of presenting practical proposals is further compounded by the fact that there is much evidence that the Holy Spirit is going to use a variety of approaches in the present and future. A third complicating factor is the fact that the experience of renewal in local congregations has been so limited, we simply do not know which principles and procedures have general validity and which are valid only for isolated situations.

One could go on indefinitely citing difficulties. Nevertheless, both pastors and laymen are pleading for help. Many have come to the point of almost complete despair. Without being cynical or bitter they recognize that what the church is now doing is really not meeting the deep needs of individuals or the desperate needs of society. They know that "something" ought to be done. But what? If what the church is now doing is not adequate, what should be changed? What should we start doing? What should be done first? What next? Their cry is for help. They want and need some practical suggestions. The preceding chapter gave suggestions related to personal and individual renewal. It is now our purpose to offer suggestions relative to the corporate life and structure of the church.

How Is a Group "On Mission" Formed?

As a background for these practical proposals, it is necessary for me to share a personal experience.

In the last chapter I told of the group of which I was a part in the early 1960s. After meeting for a number of months we began to feel some "new vitality" within our personal lives. We were deeply grateful for this. However, we realized that the purpose of our meeting together was not just for our own personal spiritual enrichment, important as this was. We recognized that our ministry was to the world, and if we simply sat and talked to each other, however meaningful that may have been for us, in reality our meeting would be as "introvert" as any of the present meetings of the church. Consequently, at one of our meetings a member said, "You know, we ought to be out on mission for God." Everyone quickly agreed, and another asked, "Well, what do you suggest we do?" Almost immediately someone proposed, "We could start a coffeehouse." (This was back in the days when it seemed the only way Christians could get out in the world was to start a coffeehouse.) This proposal was discussed at length. Some were in favor and some were not. So we dropped the matter.

A few months later someone said, "Really, we ought to be out on mission." And the inevitable question arose, "What do you suggest?" Several suggestions were made. These were all discussed, but we could not come to any agreement. So we dropped the matter. Again some months later the same issue was discussed, but we could not agree on what we should be doing "in the world." This went on until the summer of 1964. During the summer the group really got down to serious business in trying to find what ministry we could perform in the world. It seemed that we were moving ever closer to a decision. I was scheduled to leave in September of 1964 to go to Europe to study the involvement of the laity through the evangelical academies. I recall so vividly the last meeting my wife and I had with the group just prior to our going overseas. It seemed the group was just at the point of making a decision concerning how they were going to become involved in a ministry in the world. I remember thinking to myself, "Findley, you are foolish. Here you are going to Europe to *study* about lay involvement and these people are going to stay here and *do* it." But the time for my sabbatic came and my wife and I left.

When we returned to Louisville after being away for nine months, one of the first things I did was to find one of the members of the group and ask, "Tell me what the group decided. I have thought of you through all the months I have been away and have prayed daily for all of you. What did you finally decide on as your expression of ministry in the world?" His reply rocked me, "We haven't decided yet, but we are still talking about it!"

A short while later I happened to be in Washington, D.C. visiting the Church of the Saviour of which Gordon Cosby is pastor. I related to him the above experience and asked, "Gordon, how can we break out of this 'bottleneck' in which we seem to be trapped?" He said, "Findley, you are going about the forming of your small groups in the wrong way. Instead of getting a group of persons together and letting them try to decide on some mission, what you should do is identify the myriad areas of ministry that need to be performed in your community and city and then see if a group forms around one of these areas of ministry."[2]

This made great sense to me. Here was a possible strategy for a church. As I reflected on Cosby's answer, it seemed to me a pastor could preach a series of sermons on the theme, "God's Call to Mission." This might last for five to six weeks. During this time, the church staff and the members could make a list of all the possible areas of need and ministry they could think of. This list should be quite specific. Then on a given Sunday morning the list could be printed and put as an insert into the church bulletin. The minister, in his sermon, would emphasize that God "calls" each Christian to some ministry.[3] The people would then be asked to take the insert home with them and make this a matter of daily prayer for two weeks. Their prayer would be, "O God, where in the world are you calling me?"

At the end of two weeks they would be asked to turn in the in-

sert, and if they had felt a definite leading from God toward one of
the areas of ministry, this would be checked. The church staff, then,
would determine from this information if three or more people had
checked the same type of ministry. If so, they would be contacted and
formed into a group around this mission. Thus the group does not
decide on a mission, the mission decides the group. (A searching group
may become a mission group when all feel called to the same mission
but this happens very rarely.)

GOD'S CALL AND MY MISSION

The basic principle in this approach is sound, but my estimate of
the amount of time needed for this type of response was terribly
naïve. I had the impression that if a pastor in a series of sermons,
perhaps for five or six weeks, would point out that God was calling
all of his people to be ministers for him in some part of his world,
they would, for the most part, respond gladly. It seemed to me that
people were just waiting to be shown *what* to do, and if presented
with a concrete suggestion, they would respond eagerly. I was badly
mistaken. The response was usually three, four, or five rather than
thirty, forty, or fifty. The time involved was more in terms of years
than weeks. This gave me a new awareness of the truth that the
pivotal problem in renewal is personal. People with their present level
of commitment to Christ simply are unwilling to become seriously
involved with him in his world. Therefore in renewal we must first
seek to deal with persons and their relationship and commitment to
Christ.

This experience led to the surfacing of another principle that is
quite valid and important: we respond or accept a "mission" only
after a definite "call" from God. It is not something we choose; we
are chosen or appointed. We undertake our mission in fellowship with
God and under the judgment of God. A deep awareness that we are
undertaking this mission in response to a "call" from God, himself, is
the only adequate motivation that will lead us to the kind of depth
involvement needed by our kind of world.

Why is the matter of "call" so important? When we, as Christians,
"go to the world," we will not always be welcomed with open arms.
For example, in attempting to minister in a ghetto area, we symbolize
the Establishment to the people there. We represent the "haves" as
opposed to the "have nots." We are symbols of the society that has

"stood on their necks" for years. When they are honest with us, their response will range from cold, stark indifference to militant hostility. More than likely their response will not be, "How nice that these good people from the First Church have come to help us poor, benighted people." Quite likely their honest response would be more like, "Damn you! What are you getting scared of? Are you afraid that we're going to blow your nice little society apart?" Consequently, they may not respond with gratitude and thanks, they may give us the cold freeze and slam the door in our faces.

But the point is, we must go back. Regardless of what their response is, regardless of how we feel or what the weather is, we must go back again and again. Why? Because this is precisely what our Lord did for us. There was a time when all of us rejected him, when we turned our backs on him. But regardless of what we did he came back, seeking us. Not just once or twice; but he kept on coming back. Thus his coming to us was not conditioned by our response to him. It was conditioned only by our need and by his love for us.

It is true, in terms of strategy, that there are times when we do stop "going back." Jesus told the disciples that there were situations in which they should "shake the dust from their feet" (Luke 9:5). However, the principle is sound—our "going" to people in ministry is not conditioned by their response to us but by their need and God's love for them.

What, then, will be the motivation that will keep us going back regardless of response? Certainly it must be something deeper than the prodding of a pastor. Our love for and loyalty to the pastor will lead us to do some things. But if these activities begin to make serious demands on us, we rather quickly find excuses for why we "don't have time for this sort of thing." On the other hand, our loyalty to the church program also will lead us to engage in certain activities. Some of us have found that loyalty has caused many people to give quite unselfishly of themselves in service and work. Again, however, when the demands become more severe, enthusiasm tends to wane.

What motive, then, is adequate to lead people to the kind of depth involvement with others that a serious ministry necessitates? I am convinced that the only adequate motive is an awareness of a "call" from God to that particular ministry—that motive which is based on the awareness that in all of God's world, the one place where God is calling him is to this particular ministry.

One weakness with a part of our service in the past was that we

were guilty of ministering with a "light touch." We wanted to help
people if it didn't take too much time or didn't demand that we become too involved. If we could take them a basket of food or some
clothes, we were willing to help. This was fine, but it was the "light
touch." It didn't demand too much of us. To illustrate, a group in a
church decided that they ought to minister to the elderly people in a
certain nursing home. They finally enlisted enough people and worked
it around so that if only two people went once a month, no one would
have to go more than once a year! This is the "light touch." This is
not giving your life.

We are coming more and more to recognize that we have to give
people our lives. Whatever the nature of our ministry, whether it be
literacy training, tutoring, listening, or any one of a hundred things,
basically what people want and need is our lives. We have to give to
them ourselves. As a "priest," it is our lives we are to offer to God as
a "spiritual sacrifice" in behalf of a needy world (1 Pet. 2:5). It is
for "our bodies" as "living sacrifices" Paul pleaded in Romans 12:1.
After all, this is the way the gospel is communicated—through incarnation. In other words, what people are seeking from us is depth involvement—our lives with their lives—and this is very demanding.
What is a motivation that is sufficient to lead one person to give his
life to another person in ministry? A call from God—a deep awareness
that God, himself, is calling him to give his life in ministry in this
place, to this person or to these people. Motives to which the church
has traditionally appealed are no longer adequate.

How Discern God's Call?

The obvious question that arises is, how can a person discern God's
"call" to a particular ministry? There are so many areas of need. There
are so many ministries in which one is interested. From the myriad
possibilities where God is working in the world, how can a person
know whether this is the one special place to which God is "calling"
him?

This certainly is a valid question and it is a question which Christians have a responsibility to try to answer. Granted that the matter
of a "call" is something that is often quite nebulous and difficult to
discern, yet because of its immense importance in terms of motivation,
each Christian is under obligation to search for God's call with dili-
gence and care.

Fortunately, in this area, we are not left without light. The search is quite often lengthy and difficult, and God's leading may seem to be more precise for some than for others. But there are some "guidelines" that I have found to be tremendously helpful. Again I express my indebtedness to Gordon Cosby. In a lecture during a renewal conference at Southern Baptist Theological Seminary in 1964, he gave three principles that can be used as guidelines.

Principle number one: When a person discovers his calling to a place of special ministry, he will have a feeling of "Eureka! . . . this is it!" We know that "feeling" is quite subjective. For this reason a person ought to submit his "feeling" to the scrutiny of a concerned and knowledgeable group as well as ultimately to the church as a whole. The *"Eureka* feeling" means that as a person reflects on this area of ministry he says to himself, "This, really, is what I had rather do for God than anything else in the world." It is a ministry in which one can engage with exuberance and joy and say, "This really turns me on," or "This is my 'thing.' "

This *Eureka* feeling is a most important aspect in discerning God's call for another reason. Cosby pointed out that whenever a person engages in any type of action (or ministry), he obviously does so on the basis of some type of motivation. The significant thing that needs to be noted, however, is that in addition to performing the service, the individual *subconsciously communicates the motivation* that underlies the service. The person who is the recipient of the ministry not only receives the action but also, consciously or unconsciously, is aware of the motivation of the person performing the action. Thus, there is set up what may be called the "ought-overflow" tension. A person who performs a ministry primarily from a sense of "ought" (that is, "I feel I ought to do this"), unconsciously communicates this sense of "oughtness." A person who engages in a service with a fairly strong feeling of what it is costing him to do it unconsciously communicates this to the recipient. To illustrate: A teacher of a class of high school seniors is teaching primarily because he feels he ought to. He seldom gets any joy at all out of it and infrequently experiences any thrill from his teaching. So, Sunday after Sunday he talks about how wonderful God is and how exciting the Christian life is. But what is really coming through to the class is this sense of "oughtness"—that there really is little thrill in the Christian life; it is something we have to plod along and do. "I wish I weren't here and I hope you appreciate what I'm trying to do for you." The unconscious motivation that is communicated negates everything the teacher is trying to do!

On the other hand, we have seen people engage in ministry with an overwhelming sense of joy. This is called the sense of "overflow." This particular person engages in a ministry from a deep well of an awareness of the presence of God in his life and of the sheer joy of performing the ministry. They are involved in this service because it "turns them on." It comes from the overflow of their lives. Now, this motivation is also communicated. Thus in addition to the ministry, the recipient is confronted with something of the wonder, the awe, and the joy of God.

Here we need to note the relationship of "call" and "gift." The "call" or appointment of the Holy Spirit to a ministry is always in terms of one's gifts. Ours is a God of order and design. He gives gifts to men. Therefore it is obvious that his call to a particular mission or ministry will be related to and on the basis of our gifts. This is why we are able to do what we do best—we have a gift for it. This is also why we get a real sense of enjoyment and thrill (Eureka) in fulfilling our calling—we have a gift for it.

To be realistic we must recognize that there are times when we must engage in action simply on the basis of "ought." A particular job needs to be done and a sense of "ought" is the best (or only) motivation we have for doing it. Also we must confess that all of us do things from a combination of motives. That is, in every action or service there is an element of "ought" and perhaps some element of "overflow." The *Eureka* feeling means that in one's "calling" the element of "overflow" far outweighs the element of "ought." So, in seeking to determine whether a particular ministry is your calling, ask: Is this a ministry that *really* turns me on? What kind of unconscious motivation am I communicating when I do it?

Principle number two: When a person discovers his calling to a special place of ministry, he dreams fantastic dreams about it. Or, when a person discovers his "thing," possible ways of fulfilling this ministry tend to flood his mind. As he thinks about it, more things come to mind that ought to be done and he sees ways to accomplish them. This means that if a particular area is a person's "calling," he will know or be able to find ways to express it.

Principle number three: When a person discovers his "calling," he can't help but talk about it. He doesn't talk about it because he feels he "ought" to, but because he wants to because of his great interest and concern. Let me use my own experience to illustrate these three principles. I knew I had been called into the ministry (vocationally) and was quite confident that my basic vocational ministry was teaching in a seminary. However, as I became more keenly aware of "the world" and more aware that God was calling his people to "the world," I also came to feel that there was some special ministry to which God was "calling" me in addition to my basic vocation. Thus I set about to try to discern my "calling." In discussion with others and in private prayer, I searched. My problem was that I was so aware of the many areas of need in our world, and I was interested in all of them. For example, I was deeply sensitive to the desperate need for good Bible teachers. Also, my denomination often asked me to prepare curriculum materials. This is tremendously significant and time-consuming. Doing this meant that I could not do other things. I was also interested in the racial problem, and I felt the church ought to be in the forefront seeking to eliminate injustice and prejudice and assist the Negro in his efforts to become a whole human being. In addition I was interested in the youth problem and in the poverty problem. And I had become deeply concerned about the renewal of the church and what God seemed to be doing in a variety of places in our time.

So, in my own mind I went round and round in circles. I certainly couldn't do everything. Time simply didn't permit. What should I do? What was my special ministry, if any? What was my "calling"? For approximately eighteen months I struggled with these questions. It was not until December of 1967 that I found my answer while meeting in a small group with some seminary students. We were using the lectures that Gordon Cosby had delivered at the renewal conference in 1964 as the basis of our searching together. In reading one particular lecture as background for our group meeting, I ran across the three principles given above. I had heard the lecture when it was first delivered, and I had proofread the lecture prior to having it mimeographed. Furthermore, I had used it several times before in meeting with groups, but it was not until this particular time that I "saw" the principles. I like to think it was the Holy Spirit who "opened my eyes" and enabled me to see. But whatever the reason, at this moment, my "calling" became absolutely clear. One of the areas where I was having my major struggle had to do with a ministry to Negroes. I knew what I felt to be the failure of the church in this area. But I now became aware that every time I thought of ministering to Negroes, I said to myself, "I ought." My motive was a sense of "ought"! As I reflected upon this insight, it occurred to me that if I were to try to minister to these people, they would sense my feeling of "ought." In spite of all I could do, this unconsciously would come through.

With reference to the second principle, when I thought of trying to minister in the Negro community, I could never think of anything to do. Ideas and possibilities simply did not come to me. Concerning the third principle, I was interested enough to talk about it.

Then I asked myself, if I am not supposed to work with the Negro community, what really is it that I had rather do than anything else? What is it that really turns me on? Then the answer came to me— renewal in the church! This was my "calling"! This really "turns me on." It excites me more than anything else. In so far as I am able to understand myself and my motives, involvement in renewal is where I have a minimum of the sense of "oughtness" and a maximum of that nebulous thing called "overflow." Here more than any place I can minister from the sheer joy of ministering. If I could do only one thing for God, this is the one thing I would want to do. This is what I understand the *Eureka* feeling to be.

In terms of the second principle, when I think of renewal in the church, ideas of what can be done and what might be done simply flood my mind. There are ideas of what might be done on a seminary campus, through conferences in local churches, and through renewal conference centers.[4]

Finally, with reference to the third principle, this is a concern that is so near the top of my life, I simply can't help talking about it.

✓Types of Mission

This leads now to a consideration of the possible types of mission in which a person might engage. These, of course, are as broad and numerous as life itself and could be described in an infinite number of ways. I have chosen to divide them into two major categories—the Christian's "general mission" and possible "specific missions."

1. *The Individual's General Mission*

The general mission to which all Christians are called all the time is to be a minister and a witness in and through normal, daily relationships. I am aware that this will strike many as being quite trite. If it is, it is because we have made it so and have never really taken it seriously. In its essence this is what God is about and this is what we must be about. It is not trite; it is not simple; it is not easy. In all of life's relationships, we must seek to be an expression of the redeeming love of God to everyone.

Volumes could be written (and have been written) seeking to explain the depth of the meaning of this concept. I want to lift up two aspects for brief consideration as illustrative of what I mean by this general mission.

First, in our relationships we must seek to give serious expression to the deep meaning of the gospel. By our decision to become a Christian, we have said to the world we believe that Christ *is* the answer. Therefore we give our lives to God, and in becoming his child, everything we do, every relationship is a reflection upon him (just as any act of a child is a reflection upon his parent). For example, a lady is having company for dinner. She forgets something needed for the evening, and rather late in the afternoon she rushes to the supermarket. Because it is the rush hour the line at the checkout counter is long and it is moving slowly. How she stands in line is a witness to her commitment to God. Actually, we are not being a Christian just when we are doing church work. And our witness involves a lot more than talking to another about becoming a Christian.

Equally important, our commitment to God also says to the world, "I believe that God's way and God's teachings are always right and best." This means that if our commitment to God is in any way serious, then our attempt to express the reality of his teachings in the ordinary affairs and relationships of life ought to be serious. However, in spite of all our loud professions, here is an area where we Christians have not begun even to scratch the surface. To illustrate, we all would agree that fundamental in our set of Christian beliefs is the statement that our Lord said was the second great commandment, "You shall love your neighbor as yourself" (Matt. 22:39, rsv). Our profession is that we are deeply committed to this teaching.

But, how would one apply this teaching in trading automobiles? This is a fairly routine transaction in which most of us engage at one time or another. When I trade automobiles, I "love myself" to the point where I want to get the best deal possible. If I love the automobile dealer as I love myself, then I will want him to get the best deal possible. But if I really want him to get the best deal possible, why is it that I keep "dickering" with him in an effort to get him to come down twenty-five, fifty, or a hundred dollars on the price? Am I doing this because I love him or because I love me?

Certainly we need to be as clear as possible as to the correct meaning of this verse. Also we should have thought through the variety of ethical issues involved, and we need to be aware of the character of the American business system. Nevertheless, it still remains that if I really believe that this teaching states the way life ought to be lived, then either I ought to find out what it means and seek to express it, or by my failure I deny any serious commitment to the teaching.

Right or wrong, I have decided what I am going to do the next time I trade automobiles. The first question I face is whether I will let the automobile dealer know that I am going to try to "love him as I love myself." (This, of course, is in the hope that if he knows, he will "love me" in return.) In my effort to "love" him I am going to this dealer and say something like this, "I want a new car with the same optional equipment on it that my present car has. There are several things wrong with my car. Whatever the price difference between my car and the new car, I will accept it without question. Also I want to tell you that I have not been to another dealer to check on his price, and after we consummate the trade I will not go to another dealer to check on the deal I received." This is going to be my way of trying to say to the automobile dealer, I really care for you. I am not going to try to exploit you for my benefit. I want you to get a good deal, too.

As I have reflected on this, it seems to me, however, that up to this point I have put the major burden on the shoulders of the automobile dealer. That is, he may be a Christian also and he may be trying to "love me" as he "loves himself." That is, he may want me to get the best possible deal, and in so doing, in light of his total expenses, he may cut his potential profit too "thin." Therefore to cover this possibility (it is only a possibility), I have decided that when he tells me what the price difference is in our trade, I will add fifty dollars to the check. This would be my way of letting the dealer know that I want him to get a good deal.

Of course, in doing this I run quite a risk. It could be that the automobile dealer is not a Christian, or if he is, he may not have this understanding of how the Christian gives his witness in ordinary, daily relationships. There is the possibility that he has already overcharged me one or two hundred dollars. His attitude may be that he really has a "sucker" on the line. But this is a risk I must run. After all, it is only money I am losing. In this transaction I am trying to say two things. First, "I really care for you, and I'm willing to put my money where my mouth is." Second, I am saying that in the nitty-gritty relationships of life, the teachings of Jesus not only can be applied, but I believe they are always right and best. If I can give a witness to my dealer-friend in these two areas, then it is worth whatever it may have cost me.

Does this sound stupid to you? Then how does a Christian trade automobiles if he tries to love the dealer as he loves himself?

Yet, I'm still not off the hook. If I try to practice this Christian teaching in trading automobiles, what about all of my other relationships? When I go to the grocery store, I am constantly looking for bargains. I don't do this because I love the company who makes the product, but because I love me. I may go to another store and pick up an item because it is less expensive than a comparable product at the first store. I then note that it was made in a foreign country. In protest against the low wages being paid workers in that country, I decide to boycott that country's products and do not purchase the item. But then I remember, that if all Christians boycotted everything from this country, the laborers would have less work to do, and their pay would be reduced even more. I am caught up in a conflict of values. How *am I* to express genuine love for my fellow-man?

Thus the ambiguity, the complexity, the difficulty of "being a witness in daily relationships" begins to overwhelm us. That which at first seemed so trite, now that we are taking it seriously, poses problems that baffle and perplex. Yet it is precisely at these points, these relationships, where Christians should struggle for answers. These are the questions and problems that ought to be the basis of discussion in at least some of the study groups in the church, for these are the relationships that make up life.

Is our action in these relationships an affirmation or a denial of our serious commitment to God? In the past, Christians have been "good" people. By this I mean, Christians have lived up to what culture expected or demanded. Most people trade automobiles on the basis of culture expectations. We have not taken seriously the idea that we are supposed to "give a witness" by the manner in which we trade automobiles. But if my commitment to God is so deep that more than anything else in the world (more even than money) I want to *be a witness* and *give a witness* to God, then it is precisely these relationships that must become a center of focus for me, because it is here that our basic commitment is expressed. Thus, my basic calling as a Christian is to be a witness to God, and one major way in which this witness must be given is in the ordinary, everyday relationships. I must seek to demonstrate that I am committed to the way of unconditional love—to God's way.

There is a second way in which we, as Christians, are to express our "general mission"—the mission to which Christians are called all the time. God in his essence is one who cares deeply for his creation. Therefore, I must seek to live in such a way that I point to one who is beyond. I must genuinely care for others in such a way that my life says, "There really is someone who cares for you." Dr. John Claypool, in one of the first sermons he preached at Crescent Hill Baptist Church, Louisville, Kentucky, said, "What happens to you makes a difference to me." As I heard it, I remember saying to myself, "That is a nice sentiment." But as I have pondered this thought through the years, it has come to take on more and more meaning. I have come to feel that this is very close to the heart of the gospel. It is also one of the major means of evangelism! We are called to care deeply and unconditionally for others. This is what God does. This is what we are called to do.

I am convinced that one of the deep hungers of modern man is to be known and to be cared for. Regardless of a person's station in life, whether he is president of a corporation or unemployed, whether he is affluent or poverty-stricken, whether he lives in suburbia or in the ghetto, every man needs to have someone who knows and cares for him. At a time when we are in danger of an exploding population, when mass media draw people ever closer together, when we are becoming increasingly crowded into urban centers; modern man, in terms of intimate, personal relationships, is tending to become increasingly impersonal and alienated. This is what the "lonely crowd" is all about. Undoubtedly the plaintive cry of the masses is expressed in some of the modern "rock" or "soul" music—"Help, I need somebody," "All the lonely people, where do they all come from?" "Why do I live? Why do I die? Tell me why."

Everyone has problems. Everyone has needs. The desperate need of the world is for people who care. This is what the gospel is all about. God cares and cares deeply. He calls us to be a people who care and care deeply. No greater opportunity for evangelism is open to us. The world can be won by a people who are willing to care and to care deeply—who are willing to love and to love unconditionally. To be an expression of this caring love is the general mission to which all Christians are called *all of the time!* It must be repeated here . . . we do not have the motivation to give ourselves in this type of unconditional caring unless we are so committed to God that to give a witness of him is the deepest desire and basic purpose of our existence. This kind of caring goes back to the depth and quality of a person's experience with God.

2. The Individual's Specific Mission

In addition to this general mission to which we are "called" all of the time, we are also probably "called" to a specific mission. That is, there is one particular place or one major way in which we are called by God to be a minister and a witness—to be his caring person in that situation. Frankly, I am not dogmatic at this point because it may be that there are some whom God calls only to the general mission discussed above. However, it is my belief that the majority of Christians are called to a specific mission also. What are some of the major options that are open to the Christian in terms of his specific mission? I believe the Christian should find his mission in *one* of the following. He certainly must not try to do all of them. For the reader who asks, "Be specific now, what might I do?" what follows is my answer.

(1) *Through one's vocation.* Some Christians will feel called to express their mission primarily through their vocation. As a case in point, here are several lawyers in a community who want to give a witness to God by being an expression of his caring concern to people. In seeking God's leading, they concluded that his "call" was for them to minister primarily through their vocation. So they formed themselves into a "mission group" (as distinguished from a "searching group") and agreed to meet each week at whatever time and place would be most convenient.

It was decided that they would do three things at each meeting. First, they would seek to minister to each other as persons—serving as priests to each other, and in this manner carry out (or continue) the ministry of the "searching groups." They will share their own strivings and "hang-ups," but each man is to be aware constantly that in order to be God's "caring person" he must work at being spiritually "alive," and they will seek to minister to each other in this vital area. Second, each man will strive to equip himself for his own particular ministry. One way of doing this is to obtain the best books that are available to help them know the opportunities, dangers, pitfalls, and limitations they may encounter in seeking to minister through their vocation. Obviously, a regular study of the Bible will be a part of this equipping process. Third, each week they will make specific plans for the way(s) in which each will seek to express his ministry the coming week.

Quite naturally, each lawyer is going to provide the best legal counsel possible. But how can he go beyond that and, by genuinely caring and being willing to become involved in another person's life, be a witness for God to the person? For example, one lawyer might be in the midst of divorce proceedings, while another is defending a juvenile delinquent. Still another may be involved in a tense situation over the settlement of an estate. Now, in addition to being a lawyer—even a good lawyer—how is each one to be a "minister" (a witness to God) in these relationships next week?

Careful planning is one of the most important things that is done each week. Then, following the discussion and planning everything is committed to God in prayer, asking for his guidance and the presence of his Spirit. And after each meeting, they will go out and seek to be an expression of God's caring concern. When they come back together the following week, they will go through the same three areas of concern. First, they will minister to each other. If one or more in the group has gotten "clobbered," he will need the strength and support of the group. One of the men may be getting discouraged because of apparent failure. He, too, will need the support and care of his fellows. Second, they will study together for further equipping. Third, they will make specific plans for ministry the next week. Thus, week after week, the pattern continues.

To illustrate, one lawyer shared how he was using his vocation as the major means through which he was expressing his ministry for God. "My business life, too, has changed radically. I had concentrated on business law—real estate, probate, that sort of thing—but now one-third of my time is spent on divorce cases. My interest now is helping people to solve their problems, whereas before I would think about my fee and not care much about my client's personal needs.

"A very gratifying result of my change in attitude and interest was to see the enactment of legislation—it just went into effect January 1—that will allow judges in Texas to require people in Texas to obtain professional counseling during divorce proceedings.

"My part in helping to get this new law on the books consisted of some rather extensive research, which I presented to our local bar association, which in turn presented it to the state bar. As a result, I was appointed to the State Bar Committee, and, with the help of a law professor at Baylor University, I drafted the legislation which was finally enacted as an amendment to our Texas 'family code.' . . .

"What excites me in a divorce case is to have a client ask, in one way or another, 'What is the purpose of my life? I've done all I know to do, and everything has gone wrong.' Almost invariably I find that such a person has failed to make use of the resources of Christian faith."[5]

The problem of being a Christian witness (being God's caring-type person), as opposed to being simply a "good" person in one's vocation is not as easy and simple as one might suppose. All too often ministers preach about being "Christian" or being "witnesses" through one's vocation, and laymen listen to such preaching with seeming intelligence. Most of the time, however, neither one has any serious or practical understanding of what is being talked about. Answers as to *how* witnessing might be done do not come as easily. However, I am convinced that if a group of individuals are so committed to God that their basic desire is to give a witness to God and they feel "called" to give their primary witness through their vocation, God will reveal ways in which they can express their witness! This is especially true if they meet together in small groups regularly to pray and share and search together. The basic question is, do we want so much to be a witness that we are willing to engage in this kind of search in order to discover? Again the personal element comes to the forefront. We must be so committed to God that the basic concern of our lives is to join with him in his redemptive mission in the world. And we do this as God does it, by caring unconditionally for people.

The types of groups are as numerous and varied as there are vocations—secretaries, nurses, executives, farmers, filling station operators, grocerymen, etc. If there are not enough people in a given church to form a small group (four to eight) for a particular vocation, then join with some in another church or another denomination. When we are serious about the basics—being a minister and witness for God in the world—the things that divide us become increasingly small. It is possible, also, to have "mixed groups." If a sufficient number from one vocation cannot be found, those from several vocations may form a group. This may make the specific equipping for ministry more difficult, but it certainly is not impossible.

A fundamental emphasis needs to be repeated. Those who seek to express their ministry primarily through their vocation do so in response to a "call from God." Otherwise the necessary motivation will be lacking and the purpose of the group will be hazy, perhaps even lost.

(2) *Through special missions in and to the world.* Certainly not all Christians will feel called to express their ministry primarily through their vocation. There will be many who will feel "called by God" to express their mission primarily through a ministry to a certain problem or needy area in society. These areas of need may include juvenile delinquents, slum residents, rehabilitation of convicts, unwed mothers, the elderly, the industrial worker, the university student, foreign students in universities, illiterates, school dropouts and potential dropouts, those who need tutoring, etc. Wherever there is an area of need, God is working and he is calling some of his people to join with him there to seek to be an instrument of redemption both to the situation and to the individual.

For example, let's look in on a particular group (four to eight) who feels "called by God" to minister specifically to unwed mothers. One is a lawyer. Certainly he is going to seek to be "Christian" in his vocation, but in terms of where he gives his extra time and where he wants to become deeply involved, he feels a special calling to minister to these unwed mothers who so often are rejected by society. Other group members include a secretary, a housewife, a groceryman, and so on. They will decide on a convenient time and place for their weekly meeting. Their first few meetings will be spent getting to know each other on a depth level.

The pattern of each weekly meeting will be the same as that suggested for the vocational group. In the first part of the meeting they will minister to each other in terms of their own personal spiritual lives. This is a very important part of each meeting. Even though they have discovered God's "mission," they will continue to have areas in their personal lives where they need the ministry of the group. Next they will engage in serious study to begin the process of equipping themselves for their particular ministry. This group, for example, will get the best books they can find dealing with unwed mothers and will study the problem from a psychological and sociological perspective. A further study can be made of the agencies that minister to these people. And visiting these social agencies will doubtless help to convince the workers that you are not interested in the "light touch" but are willing to become deeply involved in the lives of these girls. This type of study and training goes on indefinitely. It is "equipping for the ministry." And when the group feels that they are ready to become intimately involved in this ministry, the third part of each meeting will consist of making specific plans for ministry during the following week.

Another important ministry is that of teaching illiterates in the community. A group involved in this would meet each week to equip themselves to teach illiterates how to read. Then, they would fulfill their ministry by teaching one or more persons how to read. For example, there was a wealthy lady in one city who felt this was her "calling" from God, and she was put in touch with a barber who lived in the deprived area of the city. After they had been meeting for some weeks and the man was beginning to read, he asked her, "Madam, what do I owe you for teaching me?" She replied, "You don't owe me a thing." "But," he insisted, "you don't know what this means to me. You have opened up a whole new world for me. I am beginning to read now. You don't know how grateful I am. I want to pay you." Her reply was, "Sir, there is not enough money in this city to pay me for doing this." "Then," he asked, "why in the world are you doing it?" In response, she had an opportunity to verbalize her witness.

A most satisfying area of service for an individual or a group is to foreign students who are in our colleges and universities. In a time when foreign missionary activities are being curtailed this is a magnificent opportunity that is being ignored and largely untouched—a caring ministry to the students from other countries. Our interest and care and concern must be directed to them as people—without regard to trying to "make missionaries" out of them to fill the depleted ranks. But the fact remains that if we express genuine care for these foreign students on a depth level, many may have a personal experience with Jesus Christ and become missionaries when they return to their countries.

It was reported that a survey taken a few years ago indicated foreign students had a far more negative attitude toward the United States after being here for four years of study than they had when they first arrived. This is sheer tragedy! These people came here because they chose to come here. They came here seeking something. Yet because of their loneliness, because of our neglect, because of preoccupation with our own concerns, their attitudes turned from positive to negative, from hope to despair, from love to hate. Unfortunately, too many of our churches have tried to do their "Christian duty" with the usual "light touch." The church sends a bus to the university, picks up a load of the "foreign students" and buses them down to church for a chicken supper. And after a few speeches, the students are returned to the university, and the church members breathe a sigh of relief because they have "ministered" to the foreign students. But all the rest of the year the student is miserable and lonely in his bare room.

If in a given church or community there are some people who feel that a ministry to foreign students is their calling, they should form themselves into a "mission group(s)." In their meetings they would do the three things mentioned for the other groups. They would minister to each other in terms of their own personal lives. They would equip themselves for this special ministry. In this connection they would study the religions of the world and the countries represented by the students with whom they were related. Then, they would make plans for becoming personally involved on a continuing basis as a means of showing concern for them as persons. Christianity should not be crammed down their throats. They should be genuinely cared for as persons—not simply as objects of evangelism. Yet, after relationships have been established and as sharing has been experienced in other areas of their lives, there will doubtless be opportunity to share the Christian experience as well.

If, indeed, some of these students are converted to the Christian faith, what tremendous "missionaries" they can become! When they return to their country they are accepted by their own people—not as outsiders, as are missionaries. Most of these students will go back to their countries as leaders, to assume responsible positions in business, education, and government. Their views carry weight. Christianity will not be identified in the minds of their countrymen with a few poor people in a small building on a back street. By working with foreign students in this way, we have a great opportunity to get involved personally with authentic missionary activities in their countries.

A number of churches are finding a meaningful ministry in providing tutoring for potential school dropouts. Because of this educational assistance (in addition to the personal relationships), a student is enabled to complete his high school training, receive his diploma, and get a job that will support him. Thus several things are accomplished. First, a life is saved from potential despair and possible crime. Second, by helping the individual become a producing, self-supporting member of society he isn't likely to show up on the welfare rolls. Third, in experiencing a relationship of caring love, the potential dropout may come to know in a personal way the love and care of God.

In one community a Christian social worker is seeking to train a number of couples to minister in the area of the rehabilitation of convicts. Thus the possibilities for ministry in the social realm are limitless. Wherever there is need there is an opportunity for ministry. This is one vast option which an individual must consider in seeking to discover God's call to a "special mission."

(3) *Through the institutional church.* Not everyone will feel called to express his ministry primarily through his vocation. Not everyone will feel called to express his ministry primarily through some needy area of society. Some will feel called to express their ministry primarily through the local congregation. This, too, is important.

This mission will include much of what the church is now doing—or should be doing. For example, there is the ministry of teaching. Children and adolescents who are growing up in this complex, confused world, who in their own way are searching for some kind of meaning for existence, certainly need teachers who will take them seriously. And the adults in our churches need teachers who understand the fullness of the gospel, who understand that God's basic call is to his mission (not just to be "good"), and who can help them increasingly to become a more adequate expression of the People of God. Yet if a person accepts teaching as his "mission," he should do so with as deep a sense of "call" as one who accepts a "call" to the ghetto. Teaching is what really "turns him on." This is the ministry where he gets his greatest sense of thrill and fulfillment. When he thinks of ministering for God, this is the ministry that really excites him.

If there are individuals in the church who have this deep sense of "call" to teaching, they should form themselves into groups (usually on the basis of the age group they teach—children, youth, adult). The three-fold pattern that has been suggested for all "mission groups" should be followed. In each weekly meeting, the members of the group would seek to minister to each other so that their own spiritual lives will be alive and dynamic. Second, through study, they will equip themselves for the ministry of teaching. Certainly one of the continu-

ing areas of study will be the Bible. They should be expected to have
some serious mastery of the Bible and understanding of the meaning
of the gospel—if their calling is to teach. Unfortunately in most
churches at the present time, many teachers have little knowledge
of the Holy Scriptures and all too often teaching becomes a process
of the blind leading the blind. If God has called them to this ministry,
then they are responsible for becoming equipped. In addition, this
training will include becoming increasingly proficient in how to communicate the gospel meaningfully and effectively (how to teach).
Third, the group will make plans each week for fulfilling their ministry—make specific plans for teaching on Sunday. Some churches
have tried to have a weekly teachers' meeting, yet they have had great
difficulty getting many teachers to attend. This no longer should be a
problem. If God has called them, then to meet each week with a
group to share, to search, to study, to equip, to plan, and to pray is
an absolute essential!

The question is often asked, what if a church does not have enough
teachers who feel "called" to fill all the classes? Is it better to have
more teachers, all of whom may not feel "called," teaching smaller
classes or to have fewer teachers who feel "called" teaching larger
classes? There are some ambiguous aspects to these questions that
make the answering difficult. What is meant by "smaller classes" or
"larger classes"? What age group is being considered? What is the
depth of "call" which a teacher has? To use senior highs as the sample
age group, I would rather have a teacher who was "called" teaching
a class of twenty-five than to have two smaller groups taught by
teachers who were teaching because of duty. If a teacher is teaching
from a sense of "call," his commitment would equip and enable him
to minister to this larger group. His study would be more serious;
consequently, his knowledge of the Bible and of the gospel would be
much deeper. He would be more likely to become involved with the
members in their lives during the week. Finally, the teacher who
teaches from a sense of "Eureka" rather than from a sense of "ought"
will, in unconscious ways, share and reflect the vitality of the gospel
in everything he says and does.

To be realistic, however, if I were a minister in a local church I
would not dismiss all the teachers who do not feel "called." After all,
the above statement is a subjective judgment. Whether one happens
to agree or disagree with it doesn't make it right or wrong. What is
needed is some objective, verifiable evidence! Thus I would take one

strong department that was willing to experiment and try some larger classes with teachers who felt "called." What is set up as criteria for "success" or "effectiveness" and how data is to be gathered, of course, would be highly important.

Another type of mission in which people might engage in the church is that of visitation. One of the basic ministries of the church is to seek to reach people and to bring them within the fellowship of study and worship where they might be exposed to the teaching and preaching of the Word. However, I do not believe that everyone is "called" to visit. Yet much in the life of the present church gives the impression that unless one is out visiting for the church, he is not being loyal to the church or faithful as a Christian. For example, at a typical church meeting about half of the members are absent. So those who are present are exhorted to visit the absentees. Also, they are supposed to visit prospects. Or, another case in point is when the church has a special visitation night. A long announcement is made and pressure is exerted urging everyone to come out on Thursday night to go visiting. Obviously, the leader knows that "everyone" is not going to come out on Thursday night, but he wants to make them feel guilty because they don't. If everyone in the church went out visiting, they would not have time to minister to the delinquents, to the illiterates, to the unwed mothers, to the affluent, etc. Visitation, as important as it is, is not the only thing God is doing in the world. Christians must have the time and be free to perform *their particular* ministry.

Although not all are called to visit, some are, and they should form themselves into groups. Again the threefold pattern will be followed for each weekly meeting, and they will go out weekly to perform their ministry. As a result, people are brought into the sphere of fellowship, learning, and worship. However, it must be recognized that people are also coming into this fellowship as a result of the other groups who are ministering. Important as it is a direct approach to visitation is not the only, nor perhaps even the major, approach to reaching people with the gospel or bringing them within the sphere of care and concern.

Another example of a "mission" expressed through the church is that of evangelistic visitation. Just as everyone is not called to visit, so also not everyone is called to make an "evangelistic visit" (as the term is generally used). Notice, I didn't say that not everyone is called to be a witness. He is. This ministry of redemption is what God is about, and we must be involved. What I mean to say is that not everyone is to make an evangelistic visit in the sense that he is given a person's name and visits him to give an evangelistic witness. This type of witness is exceedingly difficult. If everyone in the church were to undertake to do this, the results might be far more negative than positive. Nevertheless, although everyone in the church is not called to this ministry, some are. There are those who find their greatest thrill and sense of fulfillment in this particular type of witness (as others might find theirs in working with people in poverty), and they, too, ought to form themselves into groups. Again the threefold pattern for the weekly meetings would be followed. They would minister to each other and equip themselves for this ministry. In this equipping they certainly will want to study with great care the biblical teachings on salvation so they will not lead people to respond to a man-made approach rather than to the biblical approach to salvation. They will need also to analyze their approaches to insure that they do not manipulate people into making decisions. And finally, they will make specific plans for expressing their ministry the following week.

Thus people ought to be coming to know God in a saving relationship throughout the year as the result of the ministry of these evangelistic groups. However, it must be understood that this group is not the only one (or even the major one) that has an evangelistic concern and is expressing an evangelistic witness . . . a delinquent boy, because he found a person who cared deeply enough to become involved in his life, comes to feel that there really is a God who cares, and he gives his life to this God . . . an unwed mother finds love and acceptance and comes to believe that God also can love and accept, so she gives her life to God . . . a business executive finds love and God in the midst of the ambiguities of life. To repeat, as Christians we do not minister to people in order to manipulate them into becoming Christian. We will minister to them because they are people in need, and we will minister to them whether they ever become Christian or not. However, it is our hope that they will come to know Jesus Christ as Lord, for we believe that it is only as this happens that the individual truly becomes fully human. To paraphrase Augustine, God has made man for himself and man cannot find wholeness until he finds it in God. Those who speak and write so vigorously about "humanization" and "making man fully human" must face the fact that in ministering to man only in terms of his social, psychological, educational, and economic needs they are failing to be concerned about the *whole* man. Thus, because of the ministry of all "mission groups"—through one's vocation, through a ministry to the various needy areas of society, as well as through groups related to the church—individuals will constantly be finding the reality of God and committing their lives to him. It is essential that we not get the mistaken impression that "evangelism" is carried out wholly, or even primarily, by the groups committed to "evangelistic visitation."

There may be others who feel that their "mission" is to minister to new converts and with those who unite with the church. These will be people who are concerned over the shoddy manner in which we care for new members, and they feel called to make *reality* what we say about our church becoming involved in the lives of those who unite with the fellowship. Still others may find their "mission" in the small group ministry. Small groups may have come to be so meaningful that they want to become the nucleus around which small "searching groups" are formed in which individuals may come to find themselves, may find God at a deeper level of their lives, and may find their calling under God.

Perhaps a summary of what has been said in this chapter would be helpful. 1. God's basic call to his people is a call to mission. Thus, to be Christian is to hear and accept God's call to mission. 2. This mission is redemption—both personal and social. 3. The Christian expresses his "general mission" by seeking to be an expression of God's caring concern in his normal relationships of life. 4. In addition to this general mission, it is likely that all Christians (or certainly most Christians) also have a "special mission." 5. Christians are to discern what their particular "special mission" is in response to a "call" from God. 6. The "special mission" may be found in one of the following three major areas: (1) through one's vocation, (2) through a ministry in some needy area of society, or (3) through a ministry in the institutional church. In this discussion no attempt has been made to be exhaustive in any area—only suggestive. The possibilities for ministry are as numerous and varied as Christians' creativity and the call from God.

NOTES

1. Findley B. Edge, *A Quest for Vitality in Religion* (Nashville: Broadman, 1963), pp. 15–74.

2. Again I want to express my deep indebtedness to Gordon Cosby for the insights he has shared with me. Through personal conversations, through renewal conferences he has led on the campus of the Southern Baptist Theological Seminary, through my visits to The Church of The Saviour, I have become so imbued with his thinking that I am unable to tell what is mine and what is his.

3. In this section I am using the word *call* to express what the New Testament refers to as "appointment" on the basis of one's gifts.

4. One of these renewal centers is being developed on the campus of Southern Baptist Theological Seminary. What happens in these centers is very important. Most centers specialize in one area of ministry. It is our belief that a center must provide several different types of conferences to meet the variety of needs in today's world. Also it is my belief that there should be at least two centers in every state to make them accessible to every church in a minimum of driving time.

5. Ted M. Anderson, "Can a Man Change?" *Faith at Work* (June 1970), pp. 4–5.

CHAPTER SEVEN

The Corporate Structure
of the Church

U p to this point we have been looking at the individual Christian and his call to mission and ministry. How does what we have been saying fit in with and relate to the corporate structure of the church?

FREEDOM AND VARIETY, FLEXIBILITY AND ADAPTABILITY

The church structure, as conceived here, is characterized by freedom and variety as well as by flexibility and adaptability. It must be recognized that everyone in the church is not called to do the same thing. We have a variety of gifts and a variety of callings—all of which are important. On the basis of Scripture we should have recognized this all along. "There are many parts, yet one body. The eye cannot say to the hand, 'I have no need of you,' nor again the head to the feet, 'I have no need of you'" (1 Cor. 12:20–21, RSV).

In most churches today there is one "program" into which people are to fit. We have a stated time and place for worship. There is a stated time and place in which the Bible is to be studied. Everyone engages in training at the same time. Mission study has its own special time and place. If the emphasis of the church at a given time is on visitation, then everyone is busy with visitation. In the church program everyone is expected to do the same thing at the same time.

It is true that when the church has this type of rigid "program" it is much easier to promote and administer. All publicity can be directed into one emphasis. It is easy to determine how many members cooperate and participate. But it doesn't seem that this is the way God works. Not only that, but if the whole congregation does one thing (visitation, for example), what is to be done about all the other ministries in which God is engaged in the world? In the "emerging church" (to use Bruce Larson's and Ralph Osborne's term), the individual must be free to find and fulfill "his particular calling" under God without being a slave to rigidity and structure.

FOCUSED MINISTRY

Generally each person should have only one major mission in which he is engaged for God,[1] even though some multi-talented people could be involved effectively in more than one ministry. But, I think the general rule still holds—one major specific mission for each person.

One of the weaknesses of the church of the past was that those individuals who were willing to work were so overloaded with responsibilities they simply did not have time to do anything well. Added to this was the problem of diffusion of interest. Serious Christians are concerned about many things in today's world. They are concerned about the youth, people in poverty, the race problem, pollution, the lonely and the alienated—to mention just a few. So, what do they do? The answer, too often, is nothing! They are simply *interested* in all these things. They *talk* about the problems and *deplore* these conditions, but concrete and specific action is not forthcoming.

Yet it is not expected that the individual Christian is to take action in all these different areas. In the midst of this diffusion of interest, he needs to focus on one major ministry (in response to a "call" from God) in which he will seriously become involved and seek to make a difference. The Christian must have time to fulfill his ministry. He must have motivation sufficient to lead him to be willing to have a depth involvement. And he must be equipped to fulfill this ministry. If one is thinking of a serious involvement in and commitment to the lives of other people, he will have to say with Paul, "This *one* thing I do."

If the Christian has found and is seeking to fulfill his primary mission for God, then he shouldn't feel guilty because he is not engaged in several other activities. A person simply cannot do everything! Naturally, he hopes that those whom God is calling to various other types of mission will hear and respond to this call from God. But this is their responsibility. His responsibility is to be faithful to his own call. Likewise, it should not be necessary for him to merely attend "meetings" which are held in the church but which do not actually equip him for his specific mission.

The diffusion of ministry and the failure to have a focused ministry has been a serious weakness in the life of the church. A homely illustration might serve to clarify. The biblical imagery is to view the world as a "vineyard." Being originally from Georgia, I am not very familiar with vineyards. But I have seen many cotton patches. So, if we may view God's world as a cotton patch, this is what I see. Many of us are trying to work for God, so we run aimlessly down the rows of the cotton patch, trying to cover a lot of ground as fast as possible. We see a clump of weeds and give them a quick chop with our hoe. Then we run over a few rows and chop again at some more weeds. A great deal of time is spent just dashing around, chopping hastily wherever we go, but really not making any serious difference.

What does a focused ministry mean? It means that in all of God's cotton patch, each of us must discover which *one* of the stalks God wants us to hoe around. Then he wants us to get our hoe sharpened (become equipped) and start chopping. Someone has pointed out that a magnifying glass may be held under the sun, but if it is diffused it makes no difference. However, when the magnifying glass is held under the sun and is focused, it can start a fire. We need Christians who, because of their focused ministry, will start some fires. A person should get so involved in *one* place in such depth, expressing so much care and concern, that a difference is made.

"Come" Structures and "Go" Structures

A number of people have pointed out the fact that one of the major weaknesses in the modern church is that its life and program are built around organizations that are primarily "come" structures. That is, these structures, by their very organization, say, "If you come to us, we will help you." The preaching service says, "If you come, we will lead you in worship." The Sunday school says, "If you come to us, we will teach you about God." The training organization says, "If you come to our meeting, we will help you to become trained." The missionary organizations say, "If you come to us we will teach you about missions." But the church by its organized life has said to the world, "If you don't come to our meetings, then we have no ministry for you." This undoubtedly is one reason we place such strong emphasis on trying to get people to attend our meetings. We can do nothing for them unless they attend!

However, this approach must change. This was not the way our Lord ministered. He did not insist that people come to him. He went

to them and ministered to them where they were. In the same way
the church must not wait for people to come to it (the building).
The church (people) must go to the world. The truth of the matter
is, the masses of people are not coming to the meetings of the church.
If the church ever expects to minister in any serious way to the world,
it must be a ministry that is given to people where they are—in the
world.

Therefore, in addition to some necessary "come" structures (for
these have a valid ministry), the church in its corporate life must
develop some approaches which by their very organizational structure
are designed to be "go" structures. These are structures which, by
the very manner in which they are organized, thrust people out of
the church building to serve people in the world.

The "mission groups" discussed previously are "go" structures. They
come into existence, not for their own sake, but to meet a need in
the world. The study and equipping in which the participants engage are designed to meet this specific ministry in the world. The
plans which are made are specifically related to ministering in the
world the following week. It would be inconceivable for a "mission
group" to meet each week simply for the purpose of "discussing" the
problem. The whole idea behind the "mission group" is to "go"—to
meet people where they are, to care for people where they are, and
to minister to people where they are.

This is not to say that the church does not need or should not have
"come" structures also. It is important for Christians to come together
for corporate worship, though in the future it is not likely that all worship will take place in the church building on Sunday. Also it is important for Christians to come together for serious study, though in the future not all study will take place in the church on Sunday. This is
simply to say that the church, in its corporate structure, must also
have approaches to ministry which by their very organization are designed to move people out of the church building to minister to people in the world. We must not spend all our time trying to get people
to come to church so we can minister to them. We must minister to
them where they are and whether they ever come to church or not.[2]

The fact that the life of the church has been dominated by "come"
structures is directly related to the growing disenchantment some are
coming to feel relative to the regular meetings we have in the
churches. These meetings, too often, have tended to be introvert. We
meet together and talk about the problem; we even discuss what

might be done or what ought to be done. Then the meeting is dismissed with prayer. The following week we meet again and discuss some other problem, consider what might be done or what ought to be done, and then again close with prayer. Thus most of the meetings consist almost exclusively of "talk." Though there may be serious question whether most church members are really ready to "get involved," some of the people, at least, are becoming increasingly disillusioned with meetings where the only thing that happens is that people get together and talk!

Today church leaders know how difficult it is to motivate people to attend meetings. This problem is directly related to the "come" structure–"go" structure approach. Dr. Kenneth Chafin illustrates the problem in the following way. He compares the meetings at church with the practice sessions of a football team and points out that the depth of motivation of a football team during their practice sessions is directly related to the importance of the game to be played on Saturday. If the game on a particular Saturday is a "breather," then the coach has a real problem trying to get the players to take their practice seriously. However, if the game being played on Saturday is with their traditional rival (Army vs. Navy, Georgia vs. Georgia Tech, Texas vs. Arkansas, Southern California vs. U.C.L.A.), the motivation for practice is at its very highest. The players will give it all they have. Motivation is high! Chafin points out that the same thing is true in churches. Motivation for our meetings is directly related to the importance of the "game" being played on Saturday.

The problem in the church, however, is that we never play the "game on Saturday." We simply spend all our time practicing (that is, meeting). It is becoming increasingly difficult to get our members out to practice (meeting) because we never seriously contemplate playing the game. In fact, some members are not sure what game it is that we are playing. There would be others who wouldn't even come out for practice if they seriously thought they were expected to play on Saturday and if there was a real possibility that they might get "hurt." And others would be willing to play the "game" if it were played on our home field (namely, in church), where they feel more secure. There we have our own "referees" and play by our own rules. However, if they contemplated playing the "game" on the opponents' field (in the world—where, in fact, the game must be played), then infinitely fewer of our members would be willing to play. On the opponents' field, with their referee, playing by their rules, anything might happen. Here the Christian is completely exposed to the world. Yet it is precisely to this kind of exposure the Christian is called. "Go Structures"—this is the name of the game. This is what the game is all about.

POTENTIAL CONFLICT

In all honesty we need to face the fact that sometimes to seek to lead the church in the direction suggested here is to sow the seeds of potential conflict within the life of the church. It is quite possible that a serious conflict might arise between those who are committed to the present life of the church and those who are committed to seeking new approaches. Those who are committed to the newer approaches are usually fewer in number and are a source of irritation. This group will feel that they have discovered something which is exceedingly meaningful and that it is a much more adequate expression of the gospel. Consequently, they will be vigorous in their effort to expand their views and approaches. They will constitute a threat to the majority who are committed to the church as it is. The greater the activity and the deeper the commitment on both sides, the greater the conflict.

This makes for a very difficult decision on the part of those who are seeking what they interpret to be "new life in the church." On the one hand, they do not want to be a source of conflict or a divisive element in the life of the church. The idea that they might, even remotely, be related to a potential split within the church is abhorrent to them. But on the other hand, they have become convinced that the life of the church is seriously failing to be an expression of the People of God. They are certain that fundamental changes are called for immediately, and they would like to be a part of and an expression of these changes. However, the choice with which they are confronted is painful. Either they can maintain peace and harmony within the church and deny some of their basic convictions concerning what they feel God is doing today, or they can follow where they feel God is leading and become a potentially divisive force in the church.

There is still another area of potential conflict that needs to be noted. This is a possible conflict within the nucleus that feels it is finding "new life." Those who are serving "in the world" (that is, who are working in some area of society) may have a tendency to look askance at those who are ministering within the framework of the institutional church. They may feel that these workers are not "where the action is." And their attitude may be, "If you really wanted to 'get with it' you would be out here in the world where the going is tough." On the other hand, those who are working in the institutional church may have a tendency to feel that those who are working in society are really not working in a "spiritual" area. Their attitude is, "You really ought to be working here with us on spiritual matters rather than spending your time out there in peripheral matters." Of course, the only adequate solution here is for each group to come to have a proper appreciation of the ministry of the other.

THE SHAPE OF THE ORGANIZED CHURCH

It is not my purpose here to try to be either exhaustive or definitive in suggesting a "program" for a local congregation. In the first place, the Holy Spirit is using a variety of forms to accomplish his work in our time. Thus no proposal can ever be definitive. It can only be suggestive. In the second place, I believe that each local congregation is sufficiently unique, and, following the principles of flexibility and adaptability, each will need to find its own specific approaches to ministry. However, I would like to suggest some guidelines a church might consider in organizing its life and ministry.

The organization of the church should be a reflection of the nature and purpose of the church. Thus, to keep this in focus let me again state briefly the nature of the church as I see it. The People of God are a unique people, and the essence of their uniqueness is that they have been called by God to a redemptive mission. This redemption is both personal and social. When a person responds to the call of God, he gives himself to the "ministry" of fulfilling this personal, social redemption. Thus the People of God are so committed to him that the purpose of their lives is to be involved in the redemptive mission which God is working out in the world. They believe that what God is doing is the most important thing that is happening in the world. Therefore, they give their lives to be an instrument of causing what God is seeking to do in the world to become a reality.

1. *Worship*

If this, then, is what it means to be the Church, there are three major functions in which a local congregation ought to be engaged. First, the congregation ought to be a worshiping people. The People of God need to meet corporately to express praise and gratitude, to confess and seek forgiveness, and to seek the infilling of the Spirit of God. The experience of worship is valid and necessary in its own right. But also, continuing experiences of private and corporate worship are an absolute essential for a people "on mission." It is in these experiences that we see more clearly the vision of what God is doing and are strengthened for the performance of his particular ministry.

Numerous questions might be raised in this area. What are some new forms of worship? What about the liturgical revival? Should worship move toward being more or less liturgical? What about worship for those who engage in shift work? What is to be done when the "long weekend" becomes the norm? Should worship services be provided at times other than on Sunday? Should a church have a variety of worship services each week—one formal and liturgical, another less formal and less liturgical—and let people select the service they prefer to attend? Again, variety, flexibility, and adaptability are guidelines that should be taken seriously in answering these questions.

2. Teaching-Learning

In addition to worship, the People of God, because they are serious in their desire to know who God is, what God is doing in the world, and what they need to be doing in the world, will be a people who take seriously the matter of teaching and learning. Of these two emphases, the greater emphasis should be on learning. In the past we have placed the emphasis on teaching. This has given the impression that the primary responsibility for getting the learner to learn rested with the teacher. Thus if the learner did not learn, we felt that it was the fault of the teacher; his teaching was ineffective. This is not necessarily true.

The responsibility for learning rests with the learner. If the learner doesn't want to learn, if he is unwilling to expend some effort in order to learn, then nothing the teacher does will make much difference. The fact is at the present time many of the members come to Bible study in the church with the primary idea in mind that it is the teacher who is to act and somehow from the action of the teacher "something" will happen to them. Yet most members really have no intention of engaging in serious study. In fact, if we were to begin to have serious study in the churches and expect involvement on the part of members, many (perhaps most) would stop coming.

By our emphasis on teaching (which is important), we have given the wrong impression to the learners. We now need to place the emphasis and the responsibility for learning where it belongs—on the learner. In practice this means, along with having an emphasis on helping teachers improve their teaching, we will have an equal (or greater) emphasis on helping learners to learn.

A second practical implication is that learners will recognize the possibility of and the responsibility for learning when no teacher is present. This will take place in small learning groups that do not have any formal teacher. The group accepts responsibility for teaching and learning on its own. Likewise learning will take place as the individual engages in private study. This simply means that a person who takes seriously the fact that he is a part of the People of God and recognizes that he is called by God to be a minister "on mission" will seek to understand what this means and will equip himself for this ministry. Not to engage in this kind of study calls into question whether the person has understood the nature of God's call or has made a serious and genuine response to that call.[3]

3. On Mission

The first function, worship, relates to God. It also relates to the individual Christian in terms of his own personal spiritual life. The second function, teaching-learning, relates to the individual in terms of his growth and equipping. The third function, mission, relates to the world. Here is where the Christian becomes "a man for others." It is the world which God has invaded in Incarnation, that he is seeking to redeem. And it is the world to which we are called. We are not sent to serve the church but to the world as an instrument of redemption. Thus we are not called to attend meetings in the institutional church merely to keep certain organizations alive and growing. It is the world we are seeking to save, not the institution. The church is to lose its life, and as it does so, it will find that it has fulfilled its calling. Although there are undoubtedly other important items that might be mentioned, it seems to me that these three functions constitute the essence of what a local congregation ought to be doing and by which its effectiveness ought to be evaluated. How this mission is to be expressed is described by what has already been said about our "general mission" and our "specific mission." And the church in its organized form would be one, two, fifteen, fifty, or more small groups, each having discovered its "specific mission" in response to a "call" from God.

GROUPS "ON MISSION" RELATED TO THE CHURCH

How are these groups "on mission" related to the church? One answer might be, "They are the church." The church is not the building; it is the people. Wherever the church members are in the world during the week, there is the church.

However, reference has been made earlier to the criticism of some that having these "mission groups" meeting at different times and places tends to fragment the church. This is a criticism that must be faced, both from the perspective of the church and from the perspective of the groups. After all, the church is "one body." And, although there are "many parts," these "parts" are not dismembered and isolated from the "body." Thus in the church there needs to be a sense of unity and corporateness. On the other hand, these groups need to have a feeling that they are not isolated and alone. They certainly do not want to feel that they are rebels and have been rejected by the church, or that they are being unfaithful and disloyal to the church. It is important that they feel a part of a larger fellowship, not only "accepted" by the church but also encouraged and supported by the church. They need to feel they are the church. How can this sense of unity, this sense of corporateness, be felt both by the church and by the group?

1. *Born within the Church*

In the first place these mission groups are born within the church. They are the result of the work of the Holy Spirit. The Holy Spirit places a concern upon the heart of an individual for a particular ministry, and he discovers what he feels is his "call" from God, his "Eureka." He discusses his "call" and this area of concern with the pastor, the church staff, and/or some other appropriate group (committee) in the church. The church through its leadership must also confirm the person's "call" if it is going to encourage this mission and provide financial assistance as needed. Thus the individual and the church both must hear and confirm this "call."

If the church confirms the individual's "call," he is permitted to see if there are others whom God is also calling to this ministry. For example, a person may be given four or five minutes in one of the services to extend God's call to ascertain whether God has been speaking to any others in the congregation about this particular ministry. Or he might encourage some to join with him on a "trial" basis to see whether God really is calling them to this ministry or not. He will seek out others through personal conversation. When God extends his "call" to persons for his ministry in the world, he is not always careful about keeping his "call" within our local congregations. This will not please some because they see it as a threat to the institution.

However, the church does have the right to be concerned about "wildcat groups"—groups that are started ill-advisedly or were begun by someone who may have neurotic tendencies. This is why it is essential for these groups to be born within the church and confirmed by it.

2. Commissioned by the Church

As another means of seeking to emphasize and strengthen this sense of unity and corporateness between the church and the groups, it would be well for the church to have a commissioning service for the group. The church can decide whether this should be a relatively simple and brief part of one of the regular meetings or whether an entire worship service should be devoted to it. Certainly a liturgy should be prepared in which the congregation expresses its commitment to give support, prayer, and encouragement to the members of the group as they engage in ministry. There should also be a response from the group members in which they affirm their "call" from God to this ministry and commit themselves to seeking to be a channel of God's grace, love, care, and redemption.

A number of functions can be served by such a commissioning service. In the first place, it can be an affirmation on the part of the congregation as to the importance of the ministry in which the group is engaged. In effect, the congregation says to the group, "What you are doing is significant and we affirm you in it." In the second place, the church commits itself to the group in terms of support—financial (as it may be needed—mutually agreed on before the commissioning service), prayer, training, and sustaining. Third, it is a recognition that though the "Body" is one, yet when the church is scattered, the various "parts" (groups) are in the community, each expressing its own particular ministry.

From the perspective of the group it gives a sense of belonging, a sense of corporateness. They have a deeper sense of awareness of being the church "on mission." It gives the feeling that no matter what happens to them, they are not alone. Perhaps most important, a service of commissioning would give to the group a sense of freedom. Since the church had commissioned them to fulfill a ministry in a particular area, they must have the freedom and time to do it. Thus they should not feel guilty because they do not attend all the other institutional meetings which are not related to their own particular ministry. (Worship and study, outlined above, are foundational for their ministry and thus are not to be ignored.) And leaders in the various church organizations should not feel that these group members are being "disloyal" or "unfaithful" because they do not attend every meeting.

To fulfill a ministry, to become involved in the lives of people, to seek to be a channel of God's love and redemption demands time! Group members must be free to give the time needed to fulfill their ministry. The commissioning service is the church's affirmation that it will not interfere with this freedom by making unrelated institutional demands. This does not mean that these groups are unconcerned with or unrelated to the church as an institution. It simply means that each person must always keep in clear focus the nature of his calling under God—namely, to fulfill his mission, not to serve an organizational structure.

3. *Report to the Church*

These "groups on mission" can avoid a feeling of fragmentation and develop a sense of unity with the church by making a report to the church from time to time. However, this reporting should not be done on a regularly scheduled monthly basis. There are two primary situations that would call for a report from a group. First, if the group has experienced some major victory in its ministry, it should be shared at an appropriate meeting. This is the kind of thing that cannot be programmed or scheduled. So when it "happens," let it be told! These experiences of victory should be shared with everyone for rejoicing and encouragement. Others may be working in groups that are meeting only hardships and opposition. When they hear God has had a "breakthrough" in another group, it not only is an occasion for rejoicing with fellow Christians, but it is also an encouragement to dig in deeper and work a little harder.

It seems to me that testimonies should once again become a part of the life of our churches. I have not made a study of why the testimony fell into disrepute and was discarded, but I suspect these were three of the factors:

(1) The same persons gave the testimony every time.

(2) They gave the same testimony every time.

(3) The testimony they gave was about something that happened ten, twenty, or thirty years before.

Brother Smith would always tell how he "walked the aisle" in a tent meeting when he was a boy. However, a dynamic testimony is the sharing of what God is doing now! This is one reason the ministry of Keith Miller and Bruce Larson has been so effective. Let someone with genuine modesty and gratitude begin to tell what God has done recently in his life and you will note the whole listening audience "come alive."

The second occasion for a group's report to the church is just the opposite from the one mentioned above. If they confront a crisis in their ministry or if an individual with whom they have been working is faced with a pivotal decision in his life, this should be reported to the church and a call made for the whole congregation to join with them in prayer about the crisis or the decision. This is a situation in which the whole congregation comes to the assistance of and seeks to strengthen one of its parts.

4. Supported by the Church

These groups on mission can be integrally related to the total church because of the support given them by the church. First, as was stated earlier, they would have to be confirmed by the church if they are to be an "official" part of the life of the church. If the church is going to take some responsibility for what a group does, then it must obviously have some control over what groups will have this "official" standing. This is to keep the church from having responsibility for irresponsible individuals getting involved in some "hair-brained" undertaking. Thus the church would be responsible to and for only those groups which it has confirmed and commissioned.

The church can support these groups in several ways. First, when the group is formed there can be discussion as to whether there will be any financial needs. If there are and if the church confirms the mission of the group, the church then commits itself to support the group financially. The question of the amount of financial assistance would be agreed on in advance.

Second, the church would assist the group in getting the specific training needed for their particular ministry. This is the equipping responsibility of the pastor and church staff. However, it is not expected that the staff will have the competence to "teach" all the varied areas in which people would need training. No staff would have competence to give training in a wide assortment of services—the rehabilitation of convicts, teaching illiterates to read, ministering to handicapped children, and working with people in poverty—to name only a few possibilities. However, the pastor and staff would be responsible for helping them find the resources, books, and persons needed in their training. Basically, however, the groups would be responsible for training themselves in their ministry.

RELATED QUESTIONS

When it is suggested that groups "on mission" should constitute a major part of the organized life of the church, several questions are almost always asked. What if a person says he doesn't feel "called" to do anything? There will obviously be those in the average church. People who respond this way may mean a variety of things. Some may mean, "I recognize that I am called to a mission but at this time I do not know what that mission is. I'm trying to discover it." For these we ought to thank God and seek to give whatever help we can. Others may mean, "This is a new concept for me. I need to explore it more fully to try to understand what it really means." These, too, command our assistance. Still others may mean, "I am already doing so much work in the church I simply do not have time to add anything else, mission or not." There will be a large number in this group. For all of these, the searching group is the best place to start. Here they will search for a more clear focus for their ministry on the basis of God's "call." They need to search for their "Eureka!"

But, again, we must be realistic in terms of where our churches are at the present time. The institution, in the main, must be kept organized and functioning. Thus many (perhaps most) of those devoted members who now carry the load in the life of the church will have to assume more than one responsibility. However, *as quickly as possible* (and this should have priority), those individuals who have found their "mission" ought to be freed from other responsibilities so they will have both the freedom and the time to fulfill their mission.

There will be another group who will say they do not feel "called" to any mission. However it is stated, what they mean is, "I've got all the religion I want. I attend church on Sunday morning and I don't plan to do anything else. I 'believe' and that's enough." These people are both the victim and the product of our traditional shallow approach to Christianity. They face a spiritual problem of the highest magnitude. The problem goes back to the nature of God's basic call to a person's understanding and response to this call. These people must be led, in a spirit of deepest love and concern, to reexamine their basic relationship and response to God.

Another question often asked is, "Is it permitted for a person to 'try out' a given mission to see whether or not this might be his 'calling'?" The answer is, "Yes." Not only is this permitted, it is encouraged. Sometimes this is the only way a person can discover his "Eureka." On the other hand, after trying out a given mission, if he feels this is *not* it, he must be free to leave with no pressure from the group to stay and "help out." In fact, any member of the group should be free to leave at any time.

Does one's "call to mission" change? It certainly does. A person may be a part of a certain mission group for a year or more, then feel a definite call to some other mission. One should always seek to be sensitive to the leading of the Holy Spirit.

NOTES

1. A minister friend of mine insists that there are "housekeeping" tasks in the church in which a person can and should engage in addition to his "major mission." This would include such things as serving on a committee or some task that is not demanding as to time or energy.

2. Some denominations are devising programs with this "go" thrust and this is to be highly commended. Two words of caution must be expressed, however. There is a danger that church members with their strong tradition of "talk" behind them will simply meet together to "talk" about what ought to be done, without actually getting involved in ministry. The second danger is that those who do seek to engage in some ministry will do so only in terms of a "light touch." That is, they will simply take some clothes to people in poverty, or carry a basket of food to some who are hungry without giving of their lives to become deeply involved in the lives of these other people. The "light touch" ministry is simply not adequate. In seeking to re-

deem his world, God became deeply involved in the world—he gave his own Son. If Christians are going to be instruments of his redemption, in any serious way, they, too, must become deeply involved in the world.

3. Because teaching and learning are of such importance, I will discuss this area more fully in a special section. See pp. 182-88.

CHAPTER EIGHT

The Local Congregation As a Miniature Theological Seminary

In *The Incendiary Fellowship*, Elton Trueblood wrote, "The congregation must, accordingly, be reconstructed into the pattern of a small theological seminary with the pastor as the professor."[1] He did not amplify what was involved in this concept in terms of specifics. Since reading this statement (perhaps because of my relationship with a seminary), I have sought to ascertain what this intriguing comparison might mean in specific areas.

There is a difference between God's basic "call" (*kaleō*) to the ministry which is issued to all Christians in the "ministry of the laity" (1 Pet. 2:5, 9) and his "call" (*didōmi*-appoint) for special or professional ministry (Eph. 4:11–12). However, even if we accept the fact that there is a difference and if we are willing to overlook this distinction for purposes of discussion, a comparison between a local congregation (church) and a theological seminary can be very helpful in understanding more clearly how the corporate life of the church should be structured and expressed. Several points of similarity can be noted.

CALLED TO MINISTRY

Students come to the seminary (or to use "church" terms—they "join" the seminary or become a part of the seminary community) because they have been called to the ministry. It is this call to the ministry that causes them to "unite" with the seminary. But not only do seminary students have a "sense of call" to the ministry, they have responded to this call. In some measure, at least, they have an awareness of what is involved in accepting this ministry and giving their lives to it. This is what coming to the ministry is all about.

In the same manner an individual should "unite" with the church (become a part of the church community) because he has been "called by God into the ministry." Like the seminary student, he must have some rather clear understanding of what this involves. And he becomes a part of the local congregation because he has accepted responsibility for this ministry and is ready to give his life to it.

It should be noted that a doctrine of "Church" is involved here. What does it mean to be "Church?" The church (local congregation) is a fellowship, but it is more than a fellowship. Thus a person does not unite with the church simply to become a part of a Christian fellowship. The church is a group of "believers"; but it is more than a group of believers. Thus, one does not unite with a church simply because he "believes." The church is a group of people called into existence by God for a mission—his mission. And only those who have heard this call (a call to ministry), who understand what it means and have accepted it should rightfully be members of the local church. Of course, this does not mean that there will not be unbelievers, searchers, and others who are a part of the "fellowship" of the church, attending, studying, worshiping. But if God's basic call to his people is to mission (Exod. 19:3–8), then only those who have heard the call, understand what is involved in it, and who have accepted it are, in fact, a part of the People of God. Fuzzy thinking at this point has tended to make church membership shallow and sometimes meaningless. Until clarity comes at this point, all else is going to be hazy. Becoming a part of the church community (like becoming a part of the seminary community) is the individual's response to and acceptance of his call to the ministry.

THE MINISTRY ACCEPTED

In the seminary, students recognize that the responsibility for carrying out "the ministry" is theirs. The students do not expect the faculty to have the primary responsibility for fulfilling the ministry. The students do not see their basic responsibility as being that of listening to the lectures of the professors and in other ways trying to "support" them while they (the faculty), during the time they are not lecturing, go out to do God's work. Neither do they expect the faculty, when they are not "holding services" in the classroom to go all over Kentucky, Indiana, Ohio, and Tennessee trying to fulfill the ministry. No! Obviously the students recognize that the responsibility for fulfilling God's ministry is theirs.

This concept is ludicrous when applied to a theological seminary, but unfortunately it is not a laughing matter when it is applied to the local congregation. All too often the dominant attitude of the congregation is that the primary responsibility for fulfilling God's ministry in any given place rests upon the shoulders of the pastor and other professional members of the church staff. The members seem to feel that their responsibility is to listen to the sermons (lectures in seminary) and support the church with their money to pay "somebody" to do "the work."

On the other hand seminary students recognize that the responsibility for "the ministry" is theirs. During the week and on the weekend they are all over Kentucky and surrounding areas fulfilling their ministry. In like fashion, church members must come to recognize that the responsibility for "the ministry" is theirs. And throughout the week, where they are and in terms of their calling to a "specific mission," they must be fulfilling their ministry.

The Function of the Faculty

The function of the seminary faculty is to equip (train) the students (ministers) for their ministry. In the local church it is the function of the pastor (and other members of the church staff, if any) to equip the church members (ministers) for their ministry. Throughout the previous section I tried to emphasize the importance of the congregation having a clear understanding of their calling as ministers. In this section the emphasis is on helping the pastor and other church staff members come to a clear understanding of their calling. They are the faculty of the "local church seminary."

Individual faculty members in a theological seminary do have a personal ministry which they fulfill for God in the world. They are ministers, too. But their primary calling and function is to train the students for their ministry.[2] Faculty members by their "gifts," training, and experience have demonstrated that they have competence to train others for the ministry. But the ministry of a faculty member would be vitiated if he spent all his time involved in some ministry in the world (regardless of how fine and needed it might be) and left his teaching (equipping) function undone. In the first place, a seminary would not permit this to go on for long. And in the second place, many would feel that he was not really utilizing his full potential. If he was competent to train others, he ought to be multiplying himself by training others rather than trying to do all the work by himself.

Yet this is precisely what is happening to the pastor and other staff members—all too often. Instead of seeing their task as training others, they spend their time trying to do most of the work. Is it any wonder that God's work is not being done any more effectively than it is? The only ones who are seriously working in the "vineyard" are the "faculty members" (church staff). In too many instances, all the "students" (church members) are doing is attending class.

One final point needs to be made in this connection. Most pastors I know yearn to fulfill this calling of being an "equipper" (trainer-teacher) of the congregation. When this is mentioned to the church members, their reply is, "Well, why don't they do it?" There are two primary reasons. First, the congregation's view as to the role of the pastor does not permit him to do this. The congregation's "role expectation," as it relates to the pastor, is that he is to do the visiting of the sick, the counseling, the evangelizing, etc. In trying to carry out all the functions the congregation expects of him, the pastor simply has no time (or energy) left for fulfilling his equipping task.

In the second place, too often, the members really have no serious interest in this kind of training. In a theological seminary the students come to the professors to receive their training. That is, the professor does not go out and "beg" students to come and get trained. The students have been called by God into the ministry. In accepting this call, they recognize that training is essential. In like fashion if the members of a local congregation recognize that they have been called by God into the ministry and if they have *seriously* accepted this call, they should come to the pastor seeking the training they need to fulfill their ministry. The pastor (professor) should not have to use all types of gimmicks to cajole and pressure the members to receive the training.

A VARIETY OF MINISTRIES

Although all the students in a seminary have been called to "the ministry," they have been called to a variety of "ministries." They have been called to be pastors, ministers of education, ministers of music, missionaries, workers with university students, youth or children's workers in a local church, social workers, professors in colleges or universities. Though all are in "the ministry" there are many different ways in which this ministry is expressed.

In the local church all church members have been called by God to be "ministers." Yet there is an infinite variety of ways in which their ministry might be expressed. Some may be working with the affluent, some with the alienated, some with the handicapped, some with the elderly. There will be mission groups working in all areas of the community throughout the week.

As mentioned earlier, one weakness of the church of the past was the notion that the total membership was expected to do the same thing at the same time. We seem to have forgotten completely that God is at work in many different places doing a variety of things. And he is calling some of his people to join with Him in all these different places.

A CORE CURRICULUM

In the seminary there are both a "core" curriculum and specialized vocational courses. The "core" curriculum consists of certain areas of study which are so foundational all students are expected to have a competence in them regardless of their proposed ministry. In the local church there should be a "core" curriculum—those studies that are so foundational that all church members are expected to have a thorough grounding in these areas. I would include at least five major areas in this core curriculum—Bible, theology, church history, missions, and ethics.

SPECIALIZED COURSES

In the seminary we also have specialized courses that are designed to equip the individual for his particular ministry. There are courses designed specifically for the one who plans to preach. Some courses equip students to be ministers of education. Other courses are for those planning to engage in a music ministry. Specialized courses equip the church social worker in social case work or group work. There are courses for youth ministers or children's workers.

It is obvious that a minister needs to be trained for his own particular specialized ministry. The point emphasized here is, not every seminary student is expected to take all of the specialized vocational courses. He takes only that which equips him for his particular ministry.

In the local church, in addition to the core curriculum for all members, there is need for specialized studies designed to equip the members for the particular ministry to which each is "called." The small groups "on mission" provide this opportunity. For example, the group that is seeking to teach illiterates how to read would engage in specialized literacy training, and the group that is going to minister to juvenile delinquents would get special training for this task. In these groups, as in the seminary, the specialized training is directly related to the ministry in which one is engaged.

Likewise, in the local church all of the members are not expected to participate in all of the "training courses" which will be offered in order to equip the different groups for their specialized ministry. That is, all the church members are not expected to "take" everything! Yet, too often in the past, this was the expectation. Training was provided in some area, and the whole membership was urged to attend—and condemned if they didn't. Fortunately this has changed. The new programs in most churches provide the freedom and the stimulation for members to receive training in the area of their special "calling."

THE TEACHER SPECIALIZES

The problem of the effectiveness of teaching in our churches has been a matter of concern for a number of years. Through these years I have met with literally thousands of teachers. On the one hand, I have been impressed with their dedication and devotion to God. On the other hand, I have also been impressed with the woefully ineffective teaching being done by most of them. Bible knowledge tests, comments by class members, personal observation, dropouts from the Sunday school—evidence after evidence piles up to attest to this lack of effectiveness.

One day a couple of years ago I was musing on Trueblood's idea that the local church should be a miniature theological seminary, and I asked myself, "What would this mean in the area of teaching?" Almost immediately two ideas struck me that seem to make a lot of sense. First, it occurred to me that our present teachers are ineffective because we are asking of them an impossible task! In the curriculum series that has been used most extensively by my own denomination, the pattern for a year is as follows: in one quarter the teacher teaches from some segment of the Old Testament. The next quarter is devoted to some part of the New Testament. During the third quarter he teaches in the area of theology (doctrine). And the last quarter concentrates on the Christian life (ethics).

It is practically impossible for a professional (much less a layman) to have any serious competence in these four major disciplines. As an ordained minister and seminary professor, I would be considered a "professional," religiously speaking. Yet, it occurred to me that if I were to be asked to lead a study for a quarter on the Church Fathers, I would be lost! I simply have no competence in this area. Yet if I were forced to teach such a course and if there were a teacher's manual available, you can be certain that it would be the manual I would follow. Then we wonder why teachers stick so close to the Teacher's Helps in spite of our urging them not to do so. This is all they know! Teachers are scraping the bottom of the barrel every time they teach.

In the seminary we let a professor specialize. A professor specializes in New Testament, or Old Testament, or theology. He may teach a survey that covers the whole area of his specialization. In addition he may have one, two, or more elective courses which explore in more depth certain segments of his specialization. The professor teaches these same courses year after year. His major study is in the area of his specialization. He purchases books and builds his library in this specialization. Thus, year after year, as he studies and teaches, he builds competence. Year after year he adds bits of information and illustrations to clarify and inform. He teaches from the overflow of his life and study.

It seems to me we can never have teachers in our local churches who are really competent unless we permit them to specialize. For example, let us suppose here is a teacher who felt "called" by God to the ministry of teaching and the church confirms this "call." It would then be decided by him and the church in what area he should specialize. If he chose New Testament, he would first work out a course giving a survey of the New Testament. Later he might work up an elective on the life and ministry of Jesus. Another elective might be the Book of Romans. As in the seminary, the church would have several teachers who are specialists in New Testament, several of whom would teach survey courses, and all of whom would have a variety of electives.

The fact that the teacher accepted this ministry of teaching in response to a "call" from God means that he would take it seriously. He would be a part of a mission group with four or five other teachers (preferably in the same specialty) who also have been "called." They would meet each week. As with the other mission groups, they would do three things. (1) They would seek to minister to each other. Though they are teachers, they have problems and needs. They have "hang-ups" with their children, problems related to their jobs, anxieties and fears, doubts and religious problems. Each would share his struggle and search with the others. (2) The group would study together to become "equipped" for their calling of teaching, giving special attention to their specialization. They would study together the area of teaching. How is the gospel best communicated? How can they make their teaching "come alive"? Their study to become more effective as teachers will be a lifelong affair. (3) They would share with each other their plans for teaching next Sunday, seeking the counsel of all as to ways of trying to improve what is done. People called to the ministry of teaching must be as diligent in their weekly mission group as those who are called to minister to juvenile delinquents.

As the teacher teaches his survey course and/or his elective course(s) year after year, he will become increasingly competent. Like the seminary professor, he will purchase books to build his library in the area of his specialization. He will read and study. Whenever possible he will seek professional training—perhaps a short-term course in a seminary. Each time he teaches the course on the basis of his own study, on the basis of the questions and discussion in the class, he will increasingly develop his competency. The first time he teaches the course, it will almost inevitably be quite difficult and the content will be "thin." However, after he has taught the course for five years, he begins to build both confidence and competence. And after teaching the course for ten years, he is teaching from the overflow. Unfortunately, some of our teachers have been teaching for ten years and longer, yet they are still scraping the bottom of the barrel as they try to find something to say. This is not their fault. We have asked them to teach in so many different areas we have not let them become competent in any.

Some may object that a teacher would get tired of teaching in the same area all the time. This is an objection I can answer from my own personal experience. I have been teaching Religious Education for the past twenty-five years, and I am more excited about it now than I have ever been! Thus I have been forced to conclude that we will never have laymen who can lead in *serious* study unless we encourage them to specialize in a given area and develop a degree of competency.

This study which covers the basic core curriculum—Bible, theology, church history, missions, ethics—will correspond to what we now do in the church on Sunday morning. However, in keeping with the principle of variety and flexibility, courses will be offered at other times during the week and at a variety of places. People will elect their course of study in terms of their need and interest irrespective of age or sex. A record of the courses which the members have taken will be kept by the staff in the church office (as these records are kept for the seminary student in the registrar's office). Guidance will be given to the members as to what course(s) they ought to consider taking on the basis of what courses they have had in the immediate past. John Doe might be counseled to take a course in Old Testament since he has not had a study in this area in some time. Bill Smith and Mary Jones might be counseled to take a course in missions. The courses offered (survey courses and electives) would vary in length. Some would last for only three months. Others would last for six months or for a year. This would correspond to two hour, three hour, four hour, and five hour courses in colleges and seminaries.

An alternative to letting the individuals elect the courses they want to take, would be to let the classes remain intact and have the teacher rotate among the classes. Some feel that there is a caring ministry which the class members can express for each other when they are allowed to stay together. My own feeling is that this caring fellowship can best be done in the small groups. I also know, however, that not all members will be in a small group. Thus, to be realistic, the only care some members will get will be that expressed by and through the Bible study class. When this is the case, there is no reason why a class, in consultation with the church staff, could not decide what teacher and what course they desired for a particular time.

The type of study we are discussing here would be of a *serious* nature. The teacher would undertake his task of teaching in a serious manner and the learners would seriously undertake their task of learning by taking notes, keeping a workbook, doing outside study, etc. Unfortunately *serious* study is the exception in most classes in our churches. This would call for a whole new attitude toward study and learning on the part of most people.

Also this teaching would place the primary emphasis on the systematic study of content. Its purpose would be to enable individuals to gain a serious and comprehensive knowledge of the Christian faith in its various aspects. To be more explicit, inspiration and change in conduct would *not* be a primary purpose of this study. Granted that a serious study of the Bible, or missions, or ethics may give inspiration and may, at times, change the way a person lives. However these results would be "bonuses" of this teaching; it would not be the primary purpose. The need for inspiration would be cared for through preaching and the other worship experiences. The emphasis on change in conduct, the individual's personal spiritual growth, the continuing and increasing expression of the gospel in his daily life, and his expression of ministry and witness in the world would be cared for in the searching groups and the mission groups. It is in these groups where one is in a smaller, more intimate setting that a person can reveal the areas of his deep and personal struggles. Here he knows he is loved and accepted even if he does reveal his weaknesses and struggles. It is in this type of setting where the Bible tends to become much more personal and where change tends to take place in one's life. It is also in these groups where one's ministry is discussed and where plans are made to carry it out.

In the past we have been very naïve in our view that we ought to get "response in life" from all the organizations and meetings in our churches. Let us take as an example a person who was "faithful" in all the organizations of an average church. On Sunday morning he would come for Bible study and the teacher called for some change in his personal life. Though it was difficult he resolved he was really going to try to make this change in his life this next week. Then he went to the morning preaching service. The preacher called for "action," "involvement." So, he decided this next week he was going to do something to get "involved." Then Sunday night he came to the training meeting. There he was urged to get engaged in a project with some people in poverty. In the evening preaching service he was challenged to change some other area of his life. During the week he went to the men's meeting (or for the lady, the women's meeting) and there they insisted that he get involved in a mission project. Here are five major responses he is to make in one week!

Next week he will go to the same meetings and will be asked to make five more responses. No one really expects a person to make that many responses. Someone may reply, "Certainly, we don't expect everyone to make a response in all of these meetings. You can never tell when a person might make a response, so you call for a response in all of them. If you don't get him in one meeting, get him in another." But that is not what happens. What happens is that we ask people to do so many things, they tend not to do anything! By our multiplicity of "calls for action" we condition them to ignore these "calls." They tend simply to sit, listen, and leave. If you doubt the correctness of this analysis just recall the numerous and high "appeals for action" that have been voiced in the morning preaching services, think of the number who attended these services and heard the "call," and then consider the number who made anything like a concrete response.

However, it is necessary for us to be realistic. The pastor or staff in a local church should not undertake to change the whole teaching emphasis all at once. In the first place, most of the members are really not interested in engaging in serious study. They will want to continue what they are now doing. Secondly, we will not have many teachers who are competent and "called" to this ministry and who will desire to specialize.

So, what should be done? Start out with one experimental class. Find one teacher who feels "called" to this ministry of teaching and who desires to specialize. Set the number that will be permitted in the class. Also be sure to set some rather serious requirements for those who will be permitted in the class (such as commitment to attend, purchase book to be studied, keeping notebook, taking examination, etc.). This will keep some malcontents from coming simply because they don't like the teacher of the class where they now are. This whole approach should be made experimentally—slowly and on a small scale—to determine whether in your situation it will work or not.[3]

One final word needs to be said relative to teaching. In the past there has been considerable emphasis on small classes. Many strong points can be given in support of small classes. However, in our churches we have not been able to come up with anything like adequate teachers for these small classes. Therefore, I have come to the following conclusion: I would rather have a teacher who is teaching from a sense of "call" from God (and whose call the church has confirmed), and who, on the basis of this sense of "call" is committed to this ministry, teaching a large class than to have a teacher acting with a sense of "ought" with a small class. In the first place, I think the teaching done, even with a larger class, would be much more effective. In the second place, there is a relational aspect of the Christian faith which is "caught" and not "taught." Thus the teaching which comes through the teacher on the basis of his "Eureka" may be the most significant. This is not consciously taught. The teacher may be concentrating on "content," but this incarnational teaching, nevertheless, comes through. Incidentally, this incarnational teaching also comes through the teacher who teaches from a sense of "ought," but it is negative instead of positive. The gospel needs to be taught by "turned on" people.

CONCLUSION

Now I give one final practical suggestion. If I were pastor of an average church, considering the proposals made in this book—or any other suggestions—I would not think in terms of trying to get the whole church to change all at once. Rather I would maintain the regular program to which the church was accustomed. Then I would undertake to "open some doors" and let the "new" begin to emerge— on a small or limited scale at first. The majority of the membership would undoubtedly continue with the existing church program. I would give the best leadership possible to the present program so it would be as meaningful and effective as possible. Remember, many have "grown up" with this program, and it gives meaning to their lives.

But at the same time I would do everything possible to bring into being the *new* that must emerge if the church is to minister more effectively to individuals and to the world. Using the "steps leading to renewal" mentioned earlier, I would seek to call forth those who are searching, but would not try to get everyone in a "searching group,"— one, or two, or three groups is enough at the start. And if, at an early stage, God called one or two "mission groups" into being, I would be happy. In the area of teaching, I would start with one class.

This should not be viewed as a new program to promote! The emphasis on the personal must be kept in focus. It is God who brings renewal. It is he who must bring into being a new people. My task would be to provide stimulation and the proper climate, but I would let the new emerge at its own pace.

6

6

In looking ahead—what would be the organizational structure which would provide opportunity for the people to adopt comfortably this new approach as they seek to express their calling as the People of God? It is really very simple. First, the church would worship; therefore appropriate plans would be made for them to be a worshiping people—and this must be meaningful worship. Second, the church would study. There would be numerous times, ways, and places where study could take place—but this must be serious study. Third, the church would be "on mission." Eventually there might be two, ten, fifty, or a hundred groups, each expressing its ministry in its own way. Some would involve individuals ministering to individuals. Others would be working with groups of people or with agencies. Some groups would be working in (or seeking to change) structures of society.

All of the groups would be the People of God in the world, seeking to be loving and caring, trying to change conditions that are not in harmony with God's will and seeking to meet the needs of people—physically, economically, emotionally, educationally. Through these honest expressions of care and love, some may come to know in a personal way the fullness of the love of God as he is revealed in Jesus Christ. If the church does this, it is doing what it is called to do.

NOTES

1. Elton Trueblood, *The Incendiary Fellowship* (New York: Harper & Row, 1967), p. 45.
2. This is why Trueblood used the term *player-coach* in describing the ministry of the professional minister.
3. As an aid to churches who desire to experiment with this approach a syllabus giving a course of study of the survey of the New Testament for one year has been prepared. There is also a syllabus giving a survey of the Old Testament. Each of these outlines is about eight pages in length. These may be secured for 25 cents each if you will send us a stamped self-addressed envelope. Send to: Findley B. Edge, Southern Baptist Theological Seminary, Louisville, Kentucky, 40206.

APPENDIX

Resources for Small Groups

I. BOOKS

Reid, Clyde. *Groups Alive—Church Alive*. New York: Harper & Row, 1969.

Rogers, Carl. *On Encounter Groups*. New York: Harper & Row, 1970.

Casteel, John L., ed. *The Creative Role of Interpersonal Groups in the Church Today*. New York: Association Press, 1968.

————. *Spiritual Renewal through Personal Groups*. New York: Association Press, 1957.

Monro, Claxton, and Taegel, William S. *Witnessing Laymen Make Living Churches*. Waco, Tex.: Word Books, 1968.

Raines, Robert A. *New Life in the Church*. New York: Harper & Bros., 1961.

Parker, William, and St. Johns, Elaine. *Prayer Can Change Your Life*. Englewood Cliffs, N.J.: Prentice-Hall, Inc., 1957.

Howard, Walden, ed. *Groups That Work*. Grand Rapids: Zondervan, 1967.

Drakeford, John. *Integrity Therapy*. Nashville: Broadman, 1967.

Hendrix, John. *On Becoming a Group*. Nashville: Broadman, 1970.

Shepherd, Clovis R. *Small Groups* (Some Sociological Perspectives). San Francisco: Chandler Publishing Co., 1970.

II. A SMALL GROUP EXPERIMENT

Teague, Sam E. *The John Wesley Great Experiment—Wanted: Ten Brave Christians*. Spiritual Life Publishers, Inc., 26 Auburn Ave., N.E., Atlanta, Georgia 30303.

Morris, Danny E. *A Life That Really Matters*. Spiritual Life Publishers, Inc., 26 Auburn Ave., N.E., Atlanta, Georgia 30303.

III. GUIDANCE MATERIALS FOR USE WITH SMALL GROUPS

1. Christian Outreach, Box 115, Huntingdon Valley, Pennsylvania 19006.

   "Growth by Groups"—Basic research tools for private Bible study and small-group interaction; 12-week trial offer, $3.50 each. Complete year's program, $7.50 each.

   "Destination Dialogue"—Creative approaches to personal reflection and small-group dialogue; 12-week trial offer, $3.50 each. Complete year's program, $7.50 each.

2. The Halfway House, Box 2, Newtown, Pennsylvania 18940.

Kaleidoscope—$3.50 each
Student Kaleidoscope—$2.95 each
Man Alive—$3.95 each
Student Man Alive—$2.95 each
Groups in Action—$3.95 each
Acts Alive—$2.95 each
The Coffee House Itch—$3.50 each
Serendipity—$2.95 each

3. The Lay Renewal Foundation, Inc., 1610 LaVista Road, N.E., Atlanta, Georgia 30329.

This group has prepared a series of Christian Growth Seminars (small-group studies) which consists of three programmed sessions (two five-inch tapes) and twelve participant's response guides at a cost of $12.50. "The Ministry of the Laity" is four tapes and costs $20.00.
"Christian Involvement," "Growth through Small Groups,"
"The Reality of the Holy Spirit," "Person to Person,"
"The Ministry of the Laity."

4. Yokefellows, Inc., 209 Park Road, Burlingame, California 94010.

"New Dimensions in Spiritual Growth"—Discusses how to start and lead a Yokefellow group. Personality tests are available at nominal costs which are analyzed and returned to each individual in the group. The emphasis is on prayer therapy.

5. Faith at Work, 295 Madison Avenue, New York, New York 10017.

"52 Weeks with the Bible," Walden Howard—Fifty-two study units that will encourage depth encounter for individuals and small groups.

"Faith at Work Handbooks"—A series of eight studies for small groups. Twenty-five cents each.
(1) A Fresh Look at Conversion
(2) How to Communicate Your Faith
(3) How to Start a Group
(4) Learning to Pray
(5) How to Study the Bible
(6) How to Help Other People
(7) How to Handle Relationships
(8) How to Serve God in the World

6. Detroit Industrial Mission, 13826 West McNichols, Detroit, Michigan 48235.

"A Guide to Mission Training Groups"—A booklet that gives excellent directions for beginning a group for businessmen in which they discuss from a Christian perspective the issues which they confront in their work.

7. Booklets published by Baptist Women and Baptist Men. Each booklet is a "Mission Action Group Guide." The cost for each booklet is fifty cents. They may be purchased at a Baptist Book Store.

Mission Action Projects Guide

Mission Action Survey Guide

Mission Action Group Guide
   —Juvenile Rehabilitation
   —Internationals
   —Headliners
   —Combating Moral Problems
   —Military
   —Resort Areas
   —Nonreaders
   —Economically Disadvantaged
   —the Sick
   —Prisoner Rehabilitation
   —the Aging
   —Negroes
   —Language Groups

8. Home Mission Board, 1350 Spring St., N.W., Atlanta, Georgia 30309. "Manual for Work with Deaf"

9. Wainwright House, The Laymen's Movement, Rye, New York 10580. "Living My Religion on My Job"—An excellent guide for groups of businessmen.

10. Christian Classics suggested by Elton Trueblood. Order from Yoke-fellow Associates, 230 College Avenue, Richmond, Indiana 47374.

Donne, John. *Devotions*—$1.65
Pascal, Blaise. *Pensées*—$1.45
Kelly, Thomas. *A Testament of Devotion*—$2.00
Woolman, John. *Journal*—$1.75
Law, William. *A Serious Call*—$1.45
á Kempis, Thomas. *The Imitation of Christ*—$1.95

BIBLIOGRAPHY

Anderson, Gerald H., ed. *Christian Mission in Theological Perspective.* Nashville: Abingdon, 1967.

Ayres, Francis O. *The Ministry of the Laity.* Philadelphia: Westminster Press, 1962.

Bailey, Wilfred M., and McElvaney, William K. *Christ's Suburban Body.* Nashville: Abingdon, 1970.

Berger, Peter. *The Noise of Solemn Assemblies.* Garden City, N.Y.: Doubleday, 1961.

Berton, Pierre. *The Comfortable Pew.* Philadelphia: Lippincott, 1965.

Bow, Russell. *The Integrity of Church Membership.* Waco, Tex.: Word Books, 1968.

Casteel, John L. *The Creative Role of Interpersonal Groups in the Church Today.* New York: Association Press, 1968.

――――. *Renewal in Retreats.* New York: Association Press, 1959.

Casteel, John L., ed. *Spiritual Renewal through Personal Groups.* New York: Association Press, 1957.

Clark, Edward; Malcolmson, William L.; and Molton, Warren Lane, eds. *The Church Creative.* Nashville: Abingdon, 1967.

Conners, Kenneth W. *Stranger in the Pew.* Valley Forge: Judson, 1970.

Cooper, John Charles. *Radical Christianity and Its Sources.* Philadelphia: Westminster, 1968.

Duncombe, David C. *The Shape of the Christian Life.* Nashville: Abingdon, 1969.

Eckardt, A. Roy. *The Surge of Piety in America.* New York: Association Press, 1958.

Ernsberger, David J. *Education for Renewal.* Philadelphia: Westminster, 1965.

Fisher, Wallace E. *The Affable Enemy.* Nashville: Abingdon, 1970.

――――. *From Tradition to Mission.* Nashville: Abingdon, 1965.

――――. *Preface to Parish Renewal.* Nashville: Abingdon, 1968.

Gardner, John W. *Self-Renewal.* New York: Harper & Row, 1964

Gilkey, Langdon. *How the Church Can Minister to the World Without Losing Itself.* New York: Harper & Row, 1964.

Greeley, Andrew. *Religion in the Year Two Thousand.* New York: Sheed & Ward, 1969.

Hinson, Glenn. *The Church: Design for Survival.* Nashville: Broadman, 1967.

Howard, Walden. *Nine Roads to Renewal.* Waco, Tex.: Word Books, 1967.

Howell, Robert L. *Fish for My People.* New York: Morehouse-Barlow, 1968.

Johnson, Paul G. *Buried Alive.* Richmond, Virginia: John Knox, 1968.

Jones, E. Stanley. *The Reconstruction of the Church—on What Pattern?* Nashville: Abingdon, 1970.

Jud, Gerald. *Pilgrim's Process.* Philadelphia: United Church Press, 1967.

Knight, Walker. *Struggle for Integrity.* Waco, Tex.: Word Books, 1969.

Larson, Bruce, and Osborne, Ralph. *The Emerging Church.* Waco, Tex.: Word Books, 1970.

Lecky, Robert S., and Wright, Elliott H. *Can These Bones Live?* New York: Sheed & Ward, 1969.

Little, Sara. *Youth, World, and Church.* Richmond, Va.: John Knox, 1968.

Long, Edward L. *The Role of the Self in Conflicts and Struggle.* Philadelphia: Westminster, 1963.

Long, Robert W. *Renewing the Congregation.* Minneapolis: Augsburg, 1966.

Madsen, Paul O. *Ventures in Mission.* Friendship Press, 1968.

Magee, R. J., ed. *Call to Adventure.* Nashville: Abingdon, 1967.

Marshall, David F., ed. *Creative Ministries.* Philadelphia: United Church Press, 1968.

Marty, Martin E. *The New Shape of American Religion.* New York: Harper & Row, 1959.

———. *Second Chance for American Protestants.* New York: Harper & Row, 1963.

Maston, F. B. *The Christian, the Church, and Contemporary Problems.* Waco, Tex.: Word Books, 1968.

Metz, Donald L. *New Congregations.* Philadelphia: Westminster, 1967.

Middleton, Robert G. *Privilege and Burden.* Valley Forge, Pa.: Judson Press, 1969.

Miller, Keith. *A Second Touch.* Waco, Tex.: Word Books, 1967.

———. *The Taste of New Wine.* Waco, Tex.: Word Books, 1965.

Monro, Claxton, and Taegel, William. *Witnessing Laymen Make Living Churches.* Waco, Tex.: Word Books, 1968.

Mowry, Charles E. *The Church and the New Generation.* Nashville: Abingdon, 1969.

Mullen, Thomas J. *The Renewal of the Ministry.* Nashville: Abingdon, 1963.

O'Connor, Elizabeth. *Call to Commitment.* New York: Harper & Row, 1963.

———. *Journey Inward, Journey Outward.* New York: Harper & Row, 1968.

———. *Our Many Selves.* New York: Harper & Row, 1970.

Oden, T. C. *Beyond Revolution.* Philadelphia: Westminster, 1970.

Parker, Everett C., ed. *Crisis in the Church.* Philadelphia: United Church Press, 1968.

Parker, William R., and St. Johns, Elaine. *Prayer Can Change Your Life.* New York: Prentice-Hall, 1957.

Raines, Robert. *New Life in the Church.* New York: Harper & Row, 1961.

———. *Reshaping the Christian Life.* New York: Harper & Row, 1964.

———. *The Secular Congregation.* New York: Harper & Row, 1968.

Ramsey, William. *Cycles and Renewal.* Nashville: Abingdon, 1969.

Reed, Clyde. *Groups Alive—Church Alive.* New York: Harper & Row, 1969.

Rogers, Carl. *On Encounter Groups.* New York: Harper & Row, 1970.

Rose, Stephen C. *Alarms and Visions.* New York: Association Press, 1968.

———. *The Grassroots Church.* New York: Holt, Rinehart, & Winston, 1966.

Russell, Letty. *Christian Education in Mission*. Philadelphia: Westminster, 1967.

Schaller, Lyle E. *The Impact of the Future*. Nashville: Abingdon, 1969.

Stagg, Paul L. *The Converted Church*. Valley Forge, Pa.: Judson Press, 1967.

Thatcher, Joan. *The Church Responds*. Valley Forge: Judson, 1970.

Trueblood, Elton. *The Company of the Committed*. New York: Harper & Row, 1961.

———. *The Incendiary Fellowship*. New York: Harper & Row, 1967.

Walker, Alan. *A Ringing Call to Mission*. Nashville: Abingdon, 1966.

Walker, Daniel D. *Enemy in the Pew*. New York: Harper & Row, 1967.

Webber, George W. *The Congregation in Mission*. Nashville: Abingdon, 1964.

———. *God's Colony in Man's World*. Nashville: Abingdon, 1960.

Wieser, Thomas, ed. *Planning for Mission*. New York: The U.S. Conference for the World Council of Churches, 1966.

Wilkerson, Don, with Weiskopf, Herm. *The Gutter and the Ghetto*. Waco, Tex.: Word Books, 1969.

Williams, Colin W. *Where in the World?* New York: Office of Publications and Distribution National Council of the Churches of Christ in the U.S.A., 1963.

World Council of Churches. *The Church for Others*. Geneva: Department o˞ Studies in Evangelism, 1967.

For Further Reading . . .

Shaping Your Faith, C. W. Christian

A guidebook which explains what theology is, why it is essential to faith, and how it grows and develops out of the believer and the church. Answers such questions as: What is theology? Is it divine or human or both? Why does the church need theology? Why does the Christian need it? (#80300 hardbook; #98002 paper)

The Third World and Mission, Dennis E. Clark

How will missions in the 70s differ from the traditional mission field of the past 200 years? What attitudes need adjustment? What major policy changes are called for? Dennis Clark calls for a "fresh evaluation" of the Christian world-mission. (#80180 hardback)

The Gift of Wholeness, Hal L. Edwards

The warmly human story of a modern pilgrim in search of himself . . . and in search of God. This book will give you a refreshing and very real look at one minister and his ministry—a vulnerable, open kind of life that grows and keeps on growing. (#80377 hardback)

God Loves the Dandelions, Roger Fredrikson
Learn how this pastor and his people grew as a body in Christ. A new pastor, Fredrikson discovered leaven in his congregation. Little by little, as people began to give themselves to others, the leaven began to yield and spiritual growth occurred. This book is an experience alive with potential for you and your church. A great gift for the church library. An affirming account for a small group or class study. (#80399 hardback)

Candles in the City, G. Curtis Jones
Calls for a dramatic reordering of national and personal priorities, reminding you that the proclamation of the gospel began in the city, not in the country. In search of meaningful solutions, Dr. Jones returns for inspiration to John's addresses to the seven persecuted urban congregations in Asia Minor. (#80313 hardbook).

Feed Whose Sheep? Paul D. Lowder
Traces this young minister's struggle to accept the church which too often seemed unacceptable . . . his spiritual pilgrimage to discovering that he was part of the problem of the church . . . to being able to forgive the church for her sins. Ideal for group study. (#80317 hardback)

Full Circle, David R. Mains
Full Circle shares literally hundreds of new methods to make worship a dynamic event: team preaching, music interspersed with Scripture readings, the use of secular poems and literature, new forms of prayer, graphic arts, and movies. (#98084 paper)

The Evangelical Heritage, Bernard L. Ramm
Discovers a thread of continuity for Evangelicalism by tracing the "geography" of Evangelical theology. Suggests that Evangelicals must be students of Holy Scripture; most know the inner structure of Evangelical theology; must know their cultural climate; and must rethink the manner in which God is related to the world. (#80316 hardback)